PREACHING WITH STORYTELLING

Preaching Bible Stories
Storytelling to Illustrate Bible Teaching

Jackson Day

PREACHING WITH STORYTELLING

Preaching Bible Stories
Storytelling to Illustrate Bible Teaching

Jackson Day

ISBN 978-0-9797324-9-2

> Copyright © 2013 by Jackson Day. Permission is granted to use up to five pages of this document for non-commercial purposes provided the following copyright statement is included on all pages containing material from this document: "Preaching with Storytelling © Jackson Day." Written permission is required for all commercial uses.

Bible Storytelling Project
biblestory@pobox.com
http://biblestorytelling.org

The following books by Jackson Day are available to help improve your Bible Storytelling skills:

Old Testament Bible Stories. . . . . ISBN 978-0-9797324-0-9
New Testament Bible Stories. . . . . . . ISBN 978-0-9797324-1-6
Bible Storytelling Tools. . . . . ISBN 978-0-9797324-2-3

Other books by author:
Story Crafting: The Art of Preparing and Telling Stories. . . . . ISBN 978-0-9797324-3-0
Parable Seeds: First Sowing. . . . . . . ISBN 978-0-9797324-4-7
Quick Scripture Reference for Life-Issues. . . . . ISBN 978-0-9797324-5-4
Outlines of Great Bible Themes. . . . . ISBN 978-0-9797324-6-1

These books may be ordered from:
- Amazon.com
- barnes&noble.com
- Bible Storytelling Project

TABLE OF CONTENTS

Acknowledgments.		1
Forward.		3
Introduction to Preaching with Storytelling		5
1	Crafting a Bible Story for Telling.	17
	■ Analyze the Bible Story.	17
	■ *Worksheet*: Analysis of a Bible Story.	22
	■ Analyze a Story Comparing Different Narrations of the Same Story.	30
	■ Analyze a Story by Interlocking Facts Found in Cross-References.	40
	■ Editing Is Needed When Crafting a Story for Telling..	46
2	Meat and Vegetables of Preaching with Storytelling; Expository Bible Storytelling.	69
	■ *Worksheet*: Sermon Outline for Bible Story-Text.	72
3	Serving a Bible Story; Bible Storytelling Performance.	88
	■ God's Message Can Be Just the Bible Story.	88
	■ God's Message Can Be a Bible Story Followed by Interpretation.	89
	■ Preparing to Perform a Bible Story..	91
	■ Prepare to Avoid Common Mistakes of Literates.	91
	■ Suggestions on How to Prepare to Perform a Story..	94
	■ Performing the Story.	103
4	Story-Appetizer; Start with a Story to Initiate the Audience's Urge to Listen..	105
5	Adding Flavor with Story Spices; Spice Non-Story Texts with Story-Illustrations..	112
	■ Sources for Stories to Illustrate a Biblical Truth.	121
	■ Cautions to Take with Story-Illustrations.	124
	■ *Worksheet*: Sermon Outline for Non-Story Text.	130
6	Dessert for Bible Story-Listeners; Embellished Bible Stories.	141
7	Story-Casserole Sermon; Circle One Theme with Several Stories.	151

8	One-Dish Meal; One-Story Sermon.	174
9	Chef's Creations; Communicate Truth Through Original Stories.	180
10	Digestion Helps; Listeners' Participating Activities. . . .	191
11	Where Do Stories Come From? Sources for Stories.	207
	■ Record and Keep Story-Ideas.	213

Conclusion. 215

List of Bible Stories in Chronological Order 216
■ List of Miracles in Chronological Order. 226
■ List of Jesus' Parables. 229

ACKNOWLEDGMENTS

I understand why most authors acknowledge the help of their spouses. My wife, Doris Day, helped me with this book more than anyone else. She has been my greatest helper since we began our journey together in 1965.

I lived in Brazil for thirty-three years and I struggled to think and write in Portuguese. As a result, my English suffered. I'm challenged when it comes to grammar and spelling, and I have writer's blindness–I see what I think I wrote instead of what I actually wrote. I'm very thankful for two friends who read the draft of this book, corrected mistakes, marked what was confusing, and gave suggestions for improving the book. They are:

- Mrs. Jennifer Farris is a pastor's wife. She is a stay at home mother with three young children. She is also a writer who finds life-lessons in everyday occurrences. Her writing skills helped her spot my mistakes and to give suggestions that would improve this book.
- Mrs. Diane Grill has fifteen years of experience as a legal secretary and twenty years working in the area of accounting. She is presently the financial secretary for a law firm in central Alabama. Mrs. Grill has sharp eyes to spot spelling and grammar mistakes, and to spot words or phrases that could be misunderstood by readers.
- Al Eiland is the graphic designer who prepared the front and back covers for this book.

I'm thankful for four pastors who reviewed this book. They informed me what was hard to understand and they gave suggestions for improving the book:

- Jeff Holley has a denominational position with the Tampa Bay Baptist Association. Jeff uses Bible storytelling in both teaching and preaching, and he trains pastors and Bible teachers to do Bible storytelling.
- Cade Farris is senior pastor of a local church. Cade has six years experiences of preaching through Bible stories in chronological order in local churches.

- Chris Crain is senior pastor of a church with multiple campuses. Chris had no experience with preaching with storytelling until he read a draft of this book.
- David Fletcher is minister of education and administration in a local church. David was unfamiliar with Bible storytelling until he read a draft of this book.

I became interested in using stories to illustrate biblical preaching as soon as I began preaching in the early 1960's. I began teaching Bible storytelling around 1975. I learned most of what I know about peaching Bible stories, and using stories to illustrate biblical teaching as I struggled to teach my students. I learned from my students; I hope they learned from me.

FORWARD

All of my life, I've been on a quest to become a better communicator. As a child I was always quiet and reserved. Imagine my shock when God called me to be a pastor! My sermons and lectures have always needed "life." I went to college and seminary, but I did not find the "definitive" resource I needed to add interest and impact to my messages. This changed when I met Jack Day.

I mentioned to Jack that I pastor a traditional church in the city of Birmingham with a second campus in the suburbs. The suburban campus is contemporary--dramatically different than the original location. Connected to our ministry we have opened two additional church plants. I remarked, "Jack, I need help communicating to diverse audiences. I have seniors, singles, young couples, students, children, etc. Could your method of Bible storytelling help?"

Jack handed me a draft of this book he was writing. Within its pages I have discovered the simple and powerful method of preaching Bible stories. The principles outlined here are written so that a seasoned preacher or a new church volunteer can discover how to communicate the Bible effectively. No other book has had a greater influence upon my sermon preparation. I believe *Preaching with Storytelling* will become an effective tool for your ministry.

Chris Crain, Pastor
South Roebuck Baptist Church and North Valley Church
Birmingham/Odenville/Margaret, Alabama

Storytelling is a powerful and effective communication tool. We know this from Jesus' teaching ministry. I heard many excellent Bible expositions in my seminary chapel services, but unfortunately I forgot most of the messages I heard except for one. That message was an entire storytelling sermon. The seminary professor masterfully crafted a story where he was one of the followers of Jesus who observed the crucifixion. It was an amazing sermon that touched my heart.

In my first full-time ministry position at First Baptist Opelika, Alabama, I was privileged to be led by Steve Scoggins, who modeled excellent biblical exposition, illustration, and application. Steve followed the principle: Illustrate with a story every Scripture truth you preach. Jack Day was a member of the same church and taught our staff Bible storytelling. Steve made me responsible for Wednesday night sermon time, and for four years I did Old Testament Bible stories in chronological order. It was extremely helpful having Jack in the Wednesday night congregation and as a personal friend, coach, and mentor. I found new freedom in communicating God's Word through storytelling. Bible storytelling greatly improved my sermon illustrations and delivery. I consistently received positive feedback about my growth from the people who listened to my preaching at First Baptist Opelika.

I am now a senior pastor and I use Bible storytelling exclusively on Sunday nights and also use it on Sunday mornings when I am preaching a text that is a story. Though I am in a different church with a different culture, the fact remains that people love to learn through hearing both Bible stories and good stories that illustrate biblical truth.

Jack is a master in teaching Bible storytelling and the art of storytelling for preachers. Jack planted and pastored numerous churches in the U.S. and Brazil. He understands what it means to be a pastor and a preacher. He has written this book for all those who want to preach more like Jesus. *Preaching with Storytelling* is extremely clear and full of examples and step by step methods to become both a better Bible storyteller and sermon illustrator.

I am convinced that storytelling holds the key in communicating the Bible to the emerging generations. This book Jack has written is one I wish I would have read in seminary. If you read it, you will sharpen your skills both in Bible storytelling and storytelling for sermon illustrations, and I guarantee your congregation will notice the difference in your preaching. Most importantly more people will be able to understand and apply God's Word to their lives. May we look to the example of Jesus, the Master Storyteller, and never stop growing in our passion to communicate His truth more effectively for the glory of His name.

Your partner in the gospel,
Cade Farris, Pastor
First Baptist Church of Wedowee, Alabama

INTRODUCTION TO PREACHING WITH STORYTELLING

I was eighteen years old and a high school senior when my pastor at Hillcrest Baptist Church, Enterprise, Alabama, invited me to preach for Youth Sunday worship services. I'd been in church all my life, but had no orientation on how to preach. I spoke for five minutes and quit. I felt that God wanted me to be a preacher, but my home church didn't want to hear me preach again. I began a search that I've continued all my life – to find meaningful ways to proclaim the message of Jesus to listeners.

I keep searching to find methods to help me best communicate God's Word. However, I'm aware that the results of my preaching are not just up to me. God is free to send out his word as well as to withdraw his word. Regardless of what the preacher does, sometimes in some places the word of the Lord is rare (1Samuel 3:1).

In the time before machinery, farmers sowed seed by hand and they had to be sure that the wind was not blowing. They desired a calm, still day to sow seeds. The opposite is required for sowing God's Word. Everything depends on the blowing wind of the Holy Spirit. The Holy Spirit causes God's Word not to return empty, but to accomplish what God purposes. Like the wind, the Holy Spirit can be present or absent. Jesus said, "The wind blows wherever it pleases. You hear its sound, but you cannot tell where it comes from or where it is going. So it is with everyone born of the Spirit" (John 3:8 NIV). This book suggests meaningful ways to proclaim God's message through storytelling; however, the preacher must depend on the Holy Spirit for God's Word to be understood and received.

The speech form of the Gospel is story. Jesus was a storyteller. He always told stories when he spoke to crowds. The common people heard Jesus gladly when he told a parable, a story, a comparison. Preachers who are faithful to the Carpenter's message need to be faithful to imitate the Carpenter's storytelling approach. Tell stories so common people will listen. Jesus did not lecture using abstract language. Jesus narrated stories. The gospels of Matthew, Mark, Luke, and John are in story form. The speech form of the Gospel is story.

Preachers often tell listeners to be like Jesus. Preachers should become like Jesus and speak in stories. I'm writing this book because I'm convinced that preaching can be enhanced through the skillful use of stories. Storytelling is a vital component to preaching effectively. The thrust of this book is to give guidelines on how to use storytelling in preaching.

Nearly all Scripture, from Genesis to Revelation, flows with narrative and story. The Bible doesn't give us the doctrine of creation; it gives us the creation story. The gospels don't give us the doctrine of Jesus' incarnation; they tell the story of Jesus' birth. The Gospels don't give us the doctrine of resurrection; they give ten stories of Jesus appearing after his death on the cross. The Bible's main ingredient is not doctrine; it's story. More than 70% of the Bible is in story form. Only about 10% of the Bible uses abstract language to present doctrine. God knew what he was doing when he chose story as the primary means to communicate to people.

Abraham's descendants were storytellers who told God's stories. God's historical acts are set in the framework of stories. Jesus perfected communicating God's message in story. He told stories called *parables* every time he spoke. Jesus' parables were not illustrations to punctuate his teaching points. The parables themselves revealed the message of God. Jesus' stories painted word-pictures of farmers, sheep, seeds, pearls, fathers and sons, fishermen, unemployed workers, and dishonest servants. His stories help us understand God's kingdom and picture God as a loving parent. Jesus seldom taught in lecture form; instead, he used story form of metaphor, parable, or simile to communicate. The storytelling-preacher comes closer to gospel language than any other literary or oral communication form.

The early church was a storytelling community. The early church's typical order of worship was to gather people, to tell stories, and then to break bread. A return to biblical roots requires a return to storytelling.

The Bible narrates God's story. Faith makes us aware that Bible stories are old, old stories but they are true stories. Faith results in Bible stories becoming our story. Bible stories tell us who we are, what we are to do, and what we are to avoid doing. We tell Bible stories to declare what we believe. We listen to Bible stories to discover ourselves as we identify with characters within the story.

The Gutenberg printing press gave rise to a print culture in which reading, essentially a rational activity, dominated. Oral storytelling collapsed and rational thinking increased. Preachers began to emphasize rational, abstract thinking over storytelling. The result was that the church over-intellectualized Christianity. Preachers who primarily used abstract language to interpret Scripture, elevated the gospel where it was best understood by the highly educated. Even today, the preacher who primarily talks about conceptual and systematic theology inspires his listeners to separate thought and life, belief and practice. Abstract language makes it difficult for listeners to believe in their hearts what they confess with their lips. Abstract language helps listeners divorce religious professions from life. Stories help listeners find the connection between gospel events and day-by-day events of their lives.

Story is a living concrete language that flows from the same stream that flows through listeners' lives. Listeners place themselves in the midst of the story and take a story journey with the storyteller. Listeners struggle with the meaning of an abstract thought, but they identify with and understand the story. Listeners find abstract language boring; however, a well-told story is fun for the listeners. Well-told stories allow listeners to use their childlike powers of imagination and take a story journey with the teller. Listening to stories can be the most enjoyable and effective way to receive truth.

Followers of Jesus need to internalize the story of Israel, the story of Jesus, stories told by Jesus, and stories told by Jesus' disciples to find their own story. True discipleship happens when the story of Jesus and our story become experienced as one story. I hear of Adam and Eve being expelled from the Garden of Eden; I counter-point and consider that disobeying God leads to my experiencing undesirable consequences. I hear of Jonah running from God to avoid going to Nineveh, the land of his enemies; I counter-point my flight to avoid God's plan for me to relate to people who I don't like. I hear Jesus' story of the Parable of the Sower; I counter-point by asking myself if I'm allowing God's Word to grow in my life. I hear of Peter's many mistakes; I counter-point that if God could use impetuous Peter, he can use me. I hear of the darker sides of the Bible heroes, such as Noah, Abraham, Moses, David, and Peter. Their positive faith actions as well as their negative darker actions are told; I counter-point that I'm similar to them. I flip-flop between being faithful and unfaithful. I identify with them. Their story becomes my story.

When I was a seminary student, I gained the impression that the primary reason to study the Bible was to understand historical data and doctrine. But, as I moved toward Bible storytelling, I became convinced that the primary reason to study the Bible is to tell the stories, thereby creating an interaction between God's story and the experience of story-listeners. I desire for my listeners to experience God's story in their own lives. My goal is not for my listeners to understand doctrine analytically, but for them to interact with God's story and experience a living God. *Example*: The primary purpose of a gospel story is not to focus on the relationship between the Father, the Son, and the Holy Spirit; nor to understand the doctrine of heaven or hell; nor to understand the doctrine of the end times. The primary reason for a gospel story is to invite people into a relationship with Jesus that transforms their lives. The primary reason a preacher tells stories should be to transform lives.

The main reason I love country music is that many country music songs are stories put to music, and story-songs resonate with me, or with people I know. I filter and tweak country story-songs and adapt them to fit my own experiences or of people I know. I don't know any famous country singers, but their story-songs touch my life. It's common to hear someone say, "That's my song!" The person didn't write the song; they didn't write the music; they didn't record the song; yet the song touches their life to the extent that they identify with it.

Story-listeners describe similar experiences to me. Often when I tell a story, a listener will speak to me afterwards and describe experiences they had similar to my story-characters. When they talk about the story I told, I realize they filtered the story, tweaked it, and adapted it to fit their own experiences or situations.

A guitarist told me that if a person puts his mouth next to the "D" string of a guitar and hums the "D" pitch, the "D" string begins to vibrate. The "A" string doesn't vibrate, neither does the "G" nor the "E" string but only the "D" vibrates. The "D" string vibrates because it was created to vibrate with that tone. When stories are well-told, something inside each listener's heart begins to vibrate, because we are created for our hearts to vibrate with a story.

Imagine yourself as the leader of a group riding in a bus to a winter retreat. You have the key to unlock the door of the lodge where your group will be staying. The bus arrives at the retreat location. It's raining and it's cold. People grab their bags and run to the cabin door. They are standing outside in the cold rain and you have the key in your pocket. You have the ability to unlock the door and let people inside the warm lodge; yet, you remain standing in the rain with the key in your pocket.

Many preachers are like the leader who keeps people standing in the cold because they keep the key to the door in their pockets. By using abstract language instead of storytelling, they hold people on the cold side of a locked door. More than 70% of the Bible is in story form. Jesus never spoke without telling a story. The early church grew with believers telling stories about Jesus wherever they went. Christianity has its roots in storytelling. Preachers who take stories out of their pockets and tell them unlock the door for their listeners.

Without a good story or some dimension of storytelling that illustrates the preacher's message, sermons remain so spiritual they do listeners little earthly good. Sermons without stories are abstract, spectral, create little fire, and give off limited light. Sermons without stories may help listeners love Jesus in heaven, but they seldom invite Jesus to walk with them on earth.

The United States has entered a post-literate age where the vast majority of citizens never read for pleasure. Citizens prefer the electronic media, such as television, recordings, telephone, radio, iPad, iPhone, and the internet. In 2002, the National Endowment for the Arts and the U.S. Census Bureau published "Reading at Risk." It was the result of an intensive study which studied the literacy habits of 17,000 Americans eighteen years and older. It concluded that only slightly more than one third of all adult American males now read literature. The research considered literature as novels, short stories, poetry, or drama in any print format, including the internet. Half of American adults can read only the most basic printed material. Only one third of college graduates are proficient readers. Young adults (18-34) have declined from being those most likely to read literature in the 1980's to those least likely to read literature today. Only twenty percent of Americans bought a book last year. Young adults have entered the age of post-literate orality and are often called secondary oral communicators. They seldom read and prefer oral-visual means of learning, such as video, movies, music, drama, and social networks.

Storytelling is the most effective way to communicate to post-literates. People who depend on print for information and entertainment reach conclusions on the basis of abstract reasoning. People who depend on electronic media reach conclusions on the basis of sound, image, and story. Non-readers think in story more than in abstract logic. Our culture is undergoing an important transition time that changes the rules of communication. Storytelling is the key to communicating to post-literates.

When I was in seminary, I was taught to preach using a literate type of communication. I was taught to organize everything into an outline and use analytical statements, interpretive details, logical list and an occasional story for illustration. I was taught to use Bible stories for illustrations, and if my text was a Bible story, to interpret the story instead of telling it. Young preachers tell me that is how they are being taught today. A young preacher told me his preaching professor often said, "Don't tell stories, preach God's Word!"

Most American preachers use linear and sequential thinking that is common in printed media. Yet, our post-literate culture prefers to think in story. Post-literates refuse to listen to interpretive, philosophical, abstract, and linear reasoning. Post-literates think in story and preachers need to become storytellers. Preachers should not communicate in the way they prefer to speak; preachers need to tell stories if they want post-literate listeners to understand God's Word. Post-literates have brought about a storytelling revival, and the church needs to experience a storytelling revival.

I was twenty-nine years old when my wife and I moved to Brazil as missionaries. We arrived in Brazil and the first thing we did was to enroll in language school to learn to speak Portuguese to Brazilian listeners. It would have been easier for me to speak English; however, I did not preach or teach the Bible in the language that I preferred to speak. I learned Portuguese so I could preach and teach in the language that my listeners preferred. In the same way, preachers need to speak in story if they want post-literate listeners to understand God's Word.

The human race has lived in four communication eras:

1st Oral: The human voice was the primary form of communication in the oral era. Oral communication was used by Adam, Abraham, Israel, and Joseph.

2nd Script: The invention of the alphabet enabled people to communicate through the written word. The alphabet was in use by the time of Moses; however, only a few privileged people could read and write.

3rd Printed word: The printing press was invented by Gutenberg in the 1450's. The printing press utilized alphabetic moveable type and machinery, and made it possible for the printed word to be mass produced.

4th Electronic media: The invention of the telegraph in 1837 marked the first invasion into the world of print. Inventions that have moved this era forward include devices such as the telephone, the phonograph, the photograph, radio, movies, television, computers, VCR, DVD, iPads, iPhones, etc.

We are living in the third communication change in the history of mankind.

1st The first communication change was from an oral culture to an alphabetic and manuscript culture. Only a privileged minority was literate. The change took thousands of years.

2nd The second communication change was from the age of the alphabetic and manuscript culture to mechanism and print. The change began with the invention of the Gutenberg Press in the 1450's.

3rd The third communication change was from the literate world of print to the age of electronic communication. This change started with the invention of the telegraph in 1837. The change began to move rapidly in the 1960's with the increased popularity of television. The year 1985 is significant as the year of a major shift from the printed culture to the electronic culture. The shift is marked by it being the first year when more video cassettes were checked out/rented from video stores than there were books checked out of libraries. For the first time since the invention of the alphabet and manuscript, a new form of communication became more powerful than the written word.

Preachers today are living in the time of the greatest change of cultural communication since the formation of the church. This is the first time in the history of Christianity in which the most powerful medium of cultural communication is not writing.

I grew up on a farm in Alabama when cotton was king and summers were hot and winters were mild. However, the first church I pastored was in the high country of Colorado where ranching and saw milling were the main sources of income, and the summers were cool and the winters reached twenty degrees below zero. I was one of the highest paid preachers in the United States; I received my pay at 8,243 feet elevation. The communication culture in Colorado was different than the one of the Deep South. Our family lived in Brazil for thirty-three years. The communication culture in Brazil was different than the one in the USA. Preaching styles that communicate in one communication culture don't work in a radically different culture. Pastors need to realize that the literate culture communication style of recent history does not communicate as effectively in this new electronic communication age as it did in years past.

Highly literate people tend to interpret and explain what a story means. Highly literate preachers tend to tell part of a story, interrupt the story to explain it; tell another portion of the story, then explain that portion. They don't tell the whole story as a story and then give insights from the story afterwards. People with limited reading skills and post-literate secondary-oral communicators prefer to experience the story. Should the preacher preach the way he likes to preach, or should he preach the way people prefer to hear? The highly literate preacher needs to learn to speak in story if he wishes to communicate to today's post-literate culture.

Whenever and wherever stories are told, a chord is plucked within the understanding of the listeners. Often the story is heard by the ear, but listened by the sub-conscious mind where its deeper meaning resides. I'm convinced that the shortest road to lead a person to the truth is to tell them a story.

The vast majority of my listeners love it when I'm telling them stories. However, a couple of listeners expressed a desire for me to give them more of an academic, interpretive philosophical interpretation of the Scripture. They wanted a deeper analytical understanding of the Scripture. Jesus was a storyteller; Paul gave academic abstract interpretation to Jesus' actions and teachings. It is just as biblical to tell stories, like Jesus, that illustrate divine truths as it is to use academic abstract language, like Paul, to expound on the truth.

Storytelling works. Some preachers call the children to the front of the church and tell a story for a children's sermon. Parents and grandparents listen to the children's story as attentively as the children. People who have difficulty understanding the pastor's sermon understand his children's story. Some preachers think that stories are for children. They are for children, but stories are for everybody. Everybody loves a good story.

A picture is worth a thousand words, but a story can paint a thousand pictures on the canvas of listeners' brains.

The use of storytelling in ministry is not a recent phenomenon. In 2 Samuel 12:1-7, the author placed a secular story on the lips of the prophet Nathan when he confronted King David for committing adultery with Bathsheba, and having her husband Uriah killed in battle.

Prophet Nathan told David, "There were two men in the same town, one rich and the other poor. The rich man had many sheep and cattle, but the poor man had nothing except one little female lamb which he bought and raised. It grew up with his children. It shared his food, drank from his cup and even slept in his arms. The lamb was like a daughter to him. Now a traveler stopped to visit the rich man. But the rich man was too stingy to take one of his own sheep or cattle to feed the traveler. Instead, he took the poor man's one lamb and cooked it for his guest to eat."

David exploded with anger and told the prophet Nathan, "The man who did this deserves to die! He must pay for that lamb four times over, for his crime and his stinginess!"

Prophet Nathan told David, "You are the man! This is what the Lord, the God of Israel, says, 'I made you king over Israel; I saved you from King Saul; I gave you King Saul's daughter and other wives; I gave you both Israel and Judah. Why did you ignore the Lord's command and do this great evil? You murdered Uriah with the sword of your enemy, and you took his wife as your wife! Now the sword will never depart from your house; murder and killing will continually plague your family. Out of your own family I'm going to bring calamity upon you. I'll take your wives and give them to one who is close to you, and he'll lie with your wives in broad daylight. You did it in secret, but I'll do it to you in broad daylight with all of Israel watching.'"

David told prophet Nathan, "I've sinned against the Lord."

Nathan replied, "The Lord forgives your sin. You're not going to die for it. Your sin made the Lord's enemies lose all respect for him; therefore, the son born to you will die" (2 Samuel 12:1-14).

Jesus was a storyteller. Jesus did not say anything to the crowd without telling them a parable (Matthew 13:34).

Preaching with storytelling can be demanding and frustrating. It is demanding to find the right story to illustrate a specific Scripture lesson. It can be frustrating not being sure how the story is received by the listeners. It is frustrating to be unsure if the story gets the message across to the listeners. The storyteller is similar to a DJ at a radio station. The transmitter (storyteller) is sending out a signal (story), but to what frequency is the receiver (listener) tuned?

Jesus told a parable that may help the storytelling-preacher deal with this uncertainty. Jesus said, "The Kingdom of God is like this. A man scatters seed on the field. Both during the night when the man is asleep and during the day when he is awake, seed is sprouting and growing. The man doesn't understand how it grows. The soil produces the grain on its own accord – first the stalk, then the head, then the full kernel in the head. As soon as the grain is ripe, the man starts to reap because the harvest has come" (Mark 4:26-29).

Jesus' parable illustrates that the Kingdom of God will achieve its full development by virtue of its own hidden nature. But the parable also illustrates the nature of storytelling. The storytelling-preacher is like the farmer who scatters seeds. Stories have within themselves a life-giving nature capable of sprouting, growing and bearing fruit in listeners' lives. The storytelling-preacher doesn't understand how it happens. The farmer plants seed every year. He doesn't know if the weather will cooperate to make a bountiful crop. In the same way, the preacher should keep telling stories, even though he doesn't know if his listeners will cooperate to help the story grow. The storytelling-preacher's primary task is to tell the story. Then he can trust the story to sprout, grow and produce fruit, even though he doesn't understand how it happens.

The purpose of expository Bible preaching with storytelling is neither to entertain nor is it to make things interesting. The purpose of preaching with storytelling is to make the Bible come alive to listeners. The storytelling-preacher tells stories so his listeners hear and learn the greatest story ever told.

My Use of Cooking Terminology

I'm using cooking terminology in this book to illustrate different types of preaching with storytelling. However, I must confess, I'm not a cook; neither am I a chef. I was raised on a farm. I remember my father doing two things in the kitchen: washing his hands in the kitchen sink and eating at the kitchen table. I helped my father work outside; my mother and sister did the housework. I went to Samford University in Birmingham, Alabama. Three of us students rented a one-bedroom cottage located behind a suburban home. We agreed to take turns with the housework. Each week, one would cook, another would wash dishes, and another would clean the cottage. I was excited. I was going to learn to cook. After my second night of cooking, my cottage mates decided that I would be the permanent dishwasher. They would take turns cooking and cleaning the house.

After I married, my wife Doris preferred to do all the cooking than to taste my cooking. We had children. My wife became pregnant when our oldest son Sam was seven years old and John was five. Doris was over eight months pregnant when one night she didn't feel well, so I cooked supper for the boys and myself. The boys ate little of what I cooked. The next night, Doris was having labor pains. I again fixed supper. John looked at his supper and refused to eat. I gave John a choice, "John, you can eat your supper or get a spanking. The choice is yours."

John replied, "Daddy, I'll take the spanking."

That night, our third son Tim was born.

After that, John and Sam wanted their mother to teach them to cook so they could prepare a meal whenever she was sick.

While nobody wants to eat my cooking, I do enjoy good cooking and I've eaten at the table of enough good cooks to understand some terminology used in cooking.

CRAFTING A BIBLE STORY FOR TELLING

Analyze the Bible Story

Food must be prepared before it can be cooked. I was raised on a farm in Alabama where our family planted a garden and grew most of the vegetables we ate. We also raised cattle, chickens, and pigs to eat. Food that came out of the garden had to be prepared before it was cooked. We shucked corn, shelled butter beans, and snapped green beans.

My wife grew up in Los Angeles, California. She didn't learn to prepare fresh vegetables; she learned to open cans or frozen packages. The first year we were married, if the electricity went out, I took her out to eat. We had a gas cooking stove, but an electric can opener.

The preacher who analyzes a Bible story before he looks at commentaries and other books is similar to the person who prepares fresh vegetables. However, the preacher who begins studying a Bible story by consulting commentaries is similar to the cook who only opens canned or frozen vegetables.

The first step to crafting a Bible story for telling is to analyze the story. The expository storytelling-preacher begins preparation by analyzing the text that is a story. He studies the text as a story instead of breaking it down into minute parts in order to find ideas. My high school science class dissected frogs. A dissected frog doesn't hop. A story that is dissected loses its life as a story.

Exegetical methods that analyze a story to understand the ideas of the story will hinder the preacher's grasping the power of a story. The story needs to be analyzed as a story instead of dissected to discover ideas. The story-preacher needs to analyze the story in such a way that both he and his listeners will participate in the reality of the gospel in story. He will use exegetical methods different from the preacher who seeks to understand the gospel in idea form.

The following suggestions will help you study a Bible story as a story.

1. **Read the Bible story, reread it, then reread it again and again**

Read the biblical passage that contains the selected story several times. Read the story daily for several days, and read it in different Bible translations. Read the story aloud; this helps your memory and gives you a feeling for the story. As you read the story, try to experience the story happening as though you were actually present.

A university professor taught students preparing to become future English teachers. The professor told his students, "Never ever read a critic on a poem before you spend time reading and living with the poem for yourself." That is excellent advice for preachers who work with Bible stories. Hold off on the commentaries until you have studied the Bible story for yourself. Read the story in the Bible. Read the story in its context. Read it in different translations. Use your mind to imagine the story happening as though you were actually present. Only then should you consult commentaries.

2. **Identify the structure of the story**

   2.1 Consider the initial-situation of the Bible story

   The context establishes the initial-situation at the beginning of the story: who the key-persons are, when did the story take place, what was its historical setting, and what series of events took place beforehand that influenced the story. The initial-situation at the beginning of the story sets the scene, introduces characters and sets up the initial-problem. It establishes what was normal for the Bible characters.

   Most of the time, the background found in the text immediately preceding the Bible story gives all the information needed for the initial-situation. In some stories, the initial-situation needs to include the back-story, the story

behind the story. The back-story gives a narrative history of background information of events that were chronologically earlier than the main story. The back-story gives the history of characters or events that underlie the initial-situation at the main story's beginning. For some Bible stories, the back-story is essential for understanding the main story.
Examples:
- It would be impossible to understand David's lament over Absalom's death without the back-story of David's sin, Absalom killing his brother who had raped his sister, and Absalom's rebellion, seeking to dethrone David.
- Listeners might conclude that Jesus saw for the first time the four fishermen he invited to follow him (Matthew 4:18-22) without the back-story of Jesus' previous encounters with the fishermen found in John chapters 1 - 4. Andrew and Peter were John the Baptist's disciples. John the Baptist told them that Jesus was the Lamb of God who takes away the sins of the world. Andrew and Peter traveled with Jesus to Cana where he transformed water to wine, and traveled to Jerusalem where he visited Nicodemus, and traveled through Samaria where he visited with a woman at a well.
- The significance of Satan beginning two of Jesus' temptations with, "If you are the son of God," would be lost without the back-story of Jesus' baptism. Jesus was baptized and a voice from heaven proclaimed, "This is my beloved Son, and I'm pleased with him."
- The back-story of Peter denying he knew Jesus is necessary to understand Jesus restoring Peter in John chapter 21.

2.2 Identify the key-person or persons

Identify the most prominent person or persons in the story. Stories are about people who face problems. Identify the person who is the main character. If the story is about more than one person, then identify the main characters.

2.3 Identify the key-location

Identify the principal location where events took place.

2.4 Identify key-repetitions

Repetitions in biblical stories emphasize truths, build a climax or express strong emotions. Bible passages that come before and after the story need to be examined to determine if the chosen story repeats words, themes, facts or ideas that are emphasized in the context of the story.

2.5 Identify key-attitudes expressed in the story

Detect attitudes, feelings and emotions expressed in the story text. Stories express attitudes, feelings, values, and emotions. A story may express a positive or negative attitude. Resignation, cynicism, hostility, shock, horror, sorrow, pain, love, joy, surprise and wonder are some of the attitudes expressed through stories. The storyteller needs to determine the attitudes the Bible story expresses in order to help his listeners experience the same desired emotions.

Characters have attitudes toward themselves, other characters, certain values, events and certain issues. A character's attitudes express opinions, points of view, and slants that a character takes toward other characters and events.

2.6 Identify the initial-problem

The initial-problem is the episode that disturbs the initial-situation presented in the context or the back-story. The initial-situation shows what was normal for the Bible characters. A change event will interrupt the normal situation. The change event sets up the initial turbulence. It may be a little problem, the first point of tension; but it hints that bigger problems are coming. The initial-problem is the first sign of trouble expressed in the story. The initial-problem creates tension for the key-character(s). It brings the key-character(s) to the cliff edge of wonder, grief, anger, confusion, fear or distress. Stories usually introduce a crisis situation at the beginning, and resolve it at the ending.

2.7 Identify the sequence of events in chronological order

The initial-situation includes the initial-problem. Then follows a series of events that include something unforeseen and unpredictable. Events move from bad to worse as tension increases until there is a final result.

2.8 Identify the final-situation of the story

Stories begin with an initial-problem or need which intensifies with a series of events until a conclusion is reached that establishes a final-situation. Identify the final-situation that shows how the story ends.

3. Discover obvious life-lessons expressed by the story

Life-lessons are important truths discovered in the story that apply to lives today. Discover all the life-lessons you can find in the story. Only consult books and commentaries when you cannot find any more life-lessons on your own. Look for obvious life-lessons. Use events recorded in the Bible story to find life-lessons for present situations.

Do not look for hidden lessons. If listeners say, "I would not have found that life-lesson in that story," it's possible that God did not intend for that story to teach that life-lesson. I once heard a preacher preach on prophet Elisha multiplying the widow's oil (2 Kings 4:1-7). From the story, the preacher came up with a life-lesson on how to be filled with the Holy Spirit. There is no way that story has life-lessons on the Holy Spirit.

4. Select the life-lessons that are most important for one's listeners

Underline or otherwise mark life-lessons that are most important to communicate to one's students or listeners.

Worksheet: ANALYSIS OF A BIBLE STORY

STORY:
TEXT:

STRUCTURE:

Initial-Situation (Context): *(Events that happened before the story started that explain its background)*

Key-person(s) *(Main character(s) in this story)*

Key-location *(Where this story took place)*

Key-repetitions *(Words, themes, facts or ideas repeated during this story)*

Key-attitudes *(Attitudes, feelings and emotions expressed during this story)*

Initial-problem *(A situation that occurs at the beginning of the story that changes the events in the initial context)*

Sequence of events in chronological order *(List of what happened in the story from the beginning to the end)*

Final-situation *(How the story ends)*

LIFE-LESSONS TAUGHT BY THE STORY:
(Important truths discovered in the story that apply to our lives today)

EXAMPLE # 1: Analysis of Genesis 4:1-16

STORY: Cain and Abel
TEXT: Genesis 4:1-16

STRUCTURE OF STORY

Key-persons:
- Cain and Abel

Key-locations:
- Altars
- Field
- Land of Nod (No Man's Land)

Key-repetitions:
- Anger (4:5, 6, 8, 9, 13, 15)
- Offering (4:3, 4, 5, 6)
- Birth: Eve (3x in 4:1-2); firstborn of flock (4:4)
- Hiding/separation from God/leave God's presence: Adam and Eve (3:8) Cain (4:16)
- Blood/murder (4:8, 10, 11, 14)
- Fugitive (4:12, 14)
- Cain's face was dark with rage (4:5, 6).
- Murder: Cain killed Abel (4:8); someone might kill Cain (4:14); God protects Cain so no one would kill him (4:15).
- Punishment: God punished Adam and Eve (3:16-19); Cain (4:11-12); Cain complained about his punishment (4:13). God protected Cain from people's punishment (4:15).

Key-attitudes:
- Thankfulness of Eve toward God
- Abel's respect for God
- Cain's disrespect for God
- Resentment of Cain toward his brother and toward God
- Deceit of Cain (lying to brother & God)
- Self-pity of Cain
- Self-justification of Cain
- Fear of Cain

Initial-situation:
After disobeying God's orders, Adam and Eve were expelled from the garden.

Initial-problem:
The couple, Adam and Eve, had two children born to them.

Sequence of events:
- Eve conceived Cain, then Abel (4:1-2).
- Abel became a herdsman; Cain became a farmer (4:3).
- Cain brought an offering from the fruit of the ground; Abel brought an offering from the firstborn of his flock (4:3-4).
- God respected Abel's offering but rejected Cain's (4:5).
- Cain became angry (4:5).
- God asked Cain why he was angry and warned him of danger (4:6-7).
- Cain killed Abel (4:8).
- God confronted Cain about his murder and punished Cain (4:9-12).
- Cain complained to God about the punishment and became a fugitive (4:16).

Final-situation:
Cain went out from God's presence.

LIFE-LESSONS DISCOVERED IN THE STORY

1. Not everyone who worships God is accepted by Him. *God accepted Abel's sacrifice but rejected Cain's.*

2. The worshiper who offers God less than his best, opens the door for temptation to assault him. *Cain offered God "some" of his produce while Abel's offering was the choice cuts of the first born of his flock (4:3-7).*

3. God seeks to communicate to the person who is making wrong choices. *Cain made wrong choices, but God alerted him that his anger resulted in sin crouching at his door (4:6-7).*

4. Religion that doesn't obey God will lead a person to commit evil. *Cain had a religion, and he brought offerings to God. Cain's religion led him to reject God's Word, murder his brother and despise God's invitation to repent and receive forgiveness (4:8-16).*

5. Anger wants to dominate the person who is experiencing it; however, the tempted person should dominate his anger. *God warned Cain: "...sin is crouching at your door; it desires to have you, but you must tame it" (4:6-7). This is figurative language, that refers to a wild animal being tamed or domesticated. Anger, desirous of attacking its victim, should be dominated.*

6. One's relationship with God does not depend on someone else's relationship to God. *Abel correctly worshiped God while his brother Cain rebelled against God (4:3-7).*

7. A person's countenance reflects his heart's condition. *Cain's face reflected his anger (4:6).*

8. Uncontrolled anger hurts others. *Cain allowed his anger to control him and he killed his brother, Abel (4:8).*

9. Lamenting punishment which is the consequence of sin is not repentance. *Cain protested against his punishment for his sin, but he did not confess to his crime, nor did he admit the justice of his punishment (4:13-14).*

10. One of the consequences of sinning is the fear of punishment. *After Cain murdered his brother, he was afraid someone would kill him (4:14).*

11. God is omniscient and is aware of people's thoughts and actions. *God knew Cain was in danger of allowing his anger to dominate him, and God knew when Cain murdered his brother (4:5-9).*

*****

EXAMPLE # 2: Analysis of 2 Kings 4:1-7

STORY: The Widow's Oil

TEXT: 2 Kings 4:1-7

STRUCTURE

Key-persons:
- Widow, sons, Elisha

Key-location:
- Widow's home in Israel

Key-repetitions:
- Debt/creditor (4:1, 7)
- Jars/containers (4:3, 4, 5, 6)
- Oil (4:2, 4, 5, 6, 7)
- Shut the door (4:3, 5)
- Bring jars (4:3, 5, 6)
- Sons (4:1, 3, 6, 7)

Key-attitudes:
- Fear on the part of the widow
- Trust of the widow in the prophet
- Positive attitude toward Elisha

Initial-situation:
   The famous prophet Elijah was taken to heaven. Elijah's assistant, Elisha, became Elijah's successor. Elisha began his prophetic ministry at a time when there was war in the land.

Initial-problem:
   Elisha, the young prophet, was beginning his ministry when a widow brought her problem to him.

Sequence of events:
- Woman brings problem to Elisha.
- Elisha tells her what to do.
- She shuts the door.

- She pours the oil.
- She runs out of containers.
- The oil stops.
- She goes back to Elisha.

Final-situation:
Elisha told the widow to sell the oil, pay her debt and live on the rest.

LIFE-LESSONS DISCOVERED IN THE STORY

1. God's people sometimes face crisis.
2. Young men often die in times of war.
3. God's people should take their problems to the Lord.
4. God provides for His people's needs.
5. The head of the household should not create debts that bring problems to his family.
6. God's people should follow His orders.
7. Solutions to crisis begin with what a person has.
8. God's provisions teach families to trust him.
9. God is concerned for widows and orphans.
10. The spiritual leader should be sensitive to the needs of those in crisis.
11. The spiritual leader should be a person to whom people with problems can go to seek help.

*****

EXAMPLE # 3: Analysis of Luke 5:27-32

STORY: Jesus Calls Levi (Matthew)

TEXT: Luke 5:27-32

STRUCTURE OF STORY

Key-persons:
- Levi (Matthew) and Jesus

Key-locations:
- Galilee, tax booth, Levi's house

Key-repetitions:
- Sinful people: In the context, Peter called himself a sinful man (5:8). In the story-text, Jesus associates with sinful people (5:30); Jesus came to save the sinful people (5:32).
- Those who followed Jesus left everything to follow him (5:11, 28).
- Tax collector(s) (5:27, 29)

Key-attitudes:
- Levi's humble attitude
- Levi's willingness to obey
- Insensitivity of Pharisees
- Compassion of Jesus
- Arrogance of the Pharisees

Initial-situation:
Jesus was at the beginning of his public ministry. Jesus had performed several miracles and had called four fishermen to follow him.

Initial-problem:
Jesus invited Levi, the tax collector, to follow him. (*Tax collectors became wealthy by collaborating with the occupying Roman government and were social outcasts.*)

Sequence of events:
- Jesus invited Levi, the tax collector, to follow him (5:27).
- Levi left everything (5:28).
- Levi invited Jesus to his house (5:29).
- A large crowd of sinners and tax collectors gathered at Levi's house (5:29).
- Jewish religious leaders complained to Jesus' disciples about Jesus eating with sinners (5:30).
- Jesus responded to the religious leaders' comments by saying he came to call sinners to repentance (5:31-32).

Final-situation:
Jesus defended himself to the religious leaders by saying he came to call sinners to repentance.

LIFE-LESSONS DISCOVERED IN THE STORY

1. Followers of Jesus should be excited about their experience with Him.
2. Jesus reaches out to people who are social outcasts.
3. Some people complain when they see people excited about following Jesus.
4. Jesus came to call people who are considered by society as bad people.
5. Believers in Jesus should invite their friends to meet Jesus.
6. Sometimes religious leaders oppose God's work.
7. The prejudice of self-righteous people creates barriers that hinder people from receiving Jesus' teaching.
8. Self-righteous people find it difficult to accept a person with a known sinful past who has now come to Jesus.
9. The Christian who follows Jesus' example is more concerned with reaching the ungodly than pleasing religious people.

Analyze a Story Comparing Different Narrations of the Same Story

Some stories are repeated in more than one book of the Bible. Some stories registered in Exodus, Leviticus and Numbers are repeated in Deuteronomy. Many stories narrated in First and Second Kings are retold in First and Second Chronicles. Stories that are repeated in different books of the Old Testament are not repeated word for word. Each telling emphasizes different facts and includes details not included in the other telling.

The stories of the life of Jesus Christ are recorded in the four gospels: Matthew, Mark, Luke, and John. Matthew, Mark, and Luke relate many of the same stories. Mark has 678 verses. The contents of 606 verses found in Mark are retold by Matthew and Luke. A gospel story that is retold in more than one book of the Bible is not repeated with exactly the same words. Sometimes they abbreviate, and other times Matthew and Luke expand on Mark's contents. Each gospel gives a different emphasis to the same story. Therefore, by comparing a story retold in different books of the Bible, it is possible to acquire more details about the same event.

EXAMPLE: COMPARING DIFFERENT TELLINGS OF THE TEMPTATION OF JESUS

The story of the temptation of Jesus is found in each of the three Synoptic Gospels: Matthew 4:1-11; Mark 1:12-13; Luke 4:1-14.
- Matthew 4:1-2 and Luke 4:1 relate that Jesus was led by the Holy Spirit into the wilderness.
- Matthew 4:2, Mark 1:13 and Luke 4:2 relate that he was in the wilderness for forty days and nights when he was tempted.
- Only Mark 1:13 relates that Jesus was with wild beasts in the wilderness.
- Matthew 4:2 and Luke 4:2 relate that Jesus fasted forty days and forty nights.
- Matthew 4:3-11 and Luke 4:3-13 relate the three episodes of the temptation.

- After the temptation, Matthew 4:11 relates that the devil left Jesus and Luke 4:13 adds that when the devil had finished the three temptations, he departed until an opportune time.
- Matthew 4:11 and Mark 1:13 relate that, after the temptation, angels ministered to Jesus.
- Only Luke 4:13-14 relates that Jesus left the wilderness and returned to Galilee in the power of the Spirit.

Sequence of events of the temptations of Jesus in their chronological order:
- Jesus was led by the Spirit into the wilderness (Mt 4:1; Lk 4:1).
- Jesus was with the wild beasts (Mk 1:13).
- Jesus fasted forty days and forty nights in the wilderness (Mt 4:1-2; Lk 4:2), being tempted by Satan (Mk 1:13; Lk 4:2).
- After the forty days of fasting, Jesus became hungry (Mt 4:2; Lk 4:2).
- The three episodes of the temptation:
  - Transform stones into bread (Mt 4:3-5; Lk 4:3-4).
  - Jump from the pinnacle of the Temple (Mt 4:5-7; Lk 4:9-12).
  - Worship the devil (Mt 4:8-10; Lk 4:5-8).
- After the temptation, the devil left Jesus (Mt 4:11), departing from him until an opportune time (Lk 4:13).
- Angels came and ministered to Jesus (Mt 4:11; Mk 1:13).
- Jesus returned from the wilderness to Galilee in the power of the Spirit (Lk 4:13-14).

When analyzing a story that is told in more than one book of the Bible, make comparisons of the different narratives of the same story.

Two resources that help the story-analyst make comparisons are:

1st **Bible Cross-References.** Most published Bibles contain cross-references listed in the margins or foot of each page. The cross-references list other texts that tell the same story, express similar ideas, or use identical words. Cross-references help the student analyzing a story in one passage to interlock it with other tellings of the same story.

2nd **A Harmony of the Gospels.** A Harmony of the Gospels organizes the material of the four gospels in chronological order. Events are told in their historical sequence and different tellings of the same story are presented side-by-side in parallel columns. A harmony facilitates the comparisons of the events, views each gospel writer's special perspective on each story, and reveals different styles of each author. The purpose for the recording of the event differs among the authors; therefore, descriptions of events and words used to convey the differing purposes of the event are recorded differently in some degree.

In order to analyze a Bible story while making comparisons of different authors that tell the same narrative, follow the same plan as **ANALYSIS OF A BIBLE STORY**. For "**Text**," note each text that tells the story. For "**Sequence of events**," note the events in chronological order making a comparison of all the texts that tell the story.

EXAMPLE # 1:   Analysis of a Story Found in Multiple Texts

STORY: Temptation of Jesus in the Wilderness

TEXT: Matthew 4:1-11; Mark 1:12-13; Luke 4:1-13

STRUCTURE:

Initial-situation (_Context, includes back-story_)
The Bible gives information about the birth of Jesus, and some facts about when he was a baby and a little boy. The Bible tells about an incident when Jesus was twelve years old and went on a trip to Jerusalem. His parents thought he was lost for three days. The Bible does not narrate facts about Jesus' life from the time he was twelve until he was thirty. During this time, Jesus lived in the village of Nazareth, working as a carpenter and was unknown beyond his home town.

When Jesus was thirty, John the Baptist was popular with the multitudes. John dressed in a garment made of camel's hair with a leather belt, and ate locusts and wild honey. He was preaching and baptizing in the wilderness of Judea, and called the people to repent and make ready the way of the Lord. Those who repented of their sins were baptized. John proclaimed, "I baptize you with water; but One is coming who is mightier than I. I am not fit to untie the thong of his sandals. He will baptize you in the Holy Spirit and fire."

Jesus came to the river Jordan to be baptized by John. John resisted, saying, "I have need to be baptized by you."

Jesus answered, "Do it at this time; for in this way it is fitting for us to fulfill all righteousness."

John baptized Jesus. Jesus came up from the water and the heavens opened, and Jesus saw the Spirit of God descending as a dove, and coming upon him.

A voice out of the heavens proclaimed, "This is my beloved Son. I'm pleased with him."

Key-persons:
- Satan and Jesus

Key-location:
- Wilderness

Key-repetitions:
- Two of the three temptations began with Satan telling Jesus, "If you are the Son of God" (Mt 4:3, 6; Lk 4:3, 9).
- Jesus answered each temptation with, "It is written" and quoted an Old Testament text (Mt 4:4, 7, 10).

Key-attitudes:
- Doubt that Satan expressed that Jesus was the Son of God
- Confidence that Jesus manifested in the Scripture
- Conflict and hostility that Satan and Jesus experienced
- Physical weakness of Jesus in contrast with his strength to resist temptation

Initial-problem:
Jesus was led by the Spirit into the wilderness to be tempted by Satan (Mt 4:1).

Sequence of events:
- Jesus was led by the Spirit into the wilderness (Mt 4:1; Lk 4:1).
- Jesus fasted forty days and forty nights in the wilderness (Mt 4:2; Lk 4:2), being tempted by Satan (Mk 1:13; Lk 4:2).
- Jesus was with the wild beasts (Mk 1:13).
- After forty days of fasting, Jesus became hungry (Mt 4:2; Lk 4:2).
- The three episodes of the temptation:
  - Transform stones into bread (Mt 4:3-5; Lk 4:3-4).
  - Jump from the pinnacle of the Temple (Mt 4:5-7; Lk 4:9-12).
  - Worship the devil (Mt 4:8-10; Lk 4:5-8).
- After the temptation, the devil left Jesus (Mt 4:11). The devil departed from Jesus until an opportune time (Lk 4:13).
- Angels came and ministered to Jesus (Mt 4:11; Mk 1:13).
- Jesus returned from the wilderness to Galilee in the power of the Spirit (Lk 4:13-14).

Final-situation:
After the temptation, Jesus returned from the wilderness to Galilee in the power of the Spirit (Mt 4:11; Mk 1:13).

LIFE-LESSONS TAUGHT BY THE STORY:

1. Satan is a lying and deceiving tempter who fights against God and his will. *He tempted Jesus to rebel against God as he had tempted Adam and Eve.*

2. The person who has faith in God does not need to prove his position with God. *God the Father called Jesus "My Son" (Mt 3:17). Satan challenged Jesus to prove he was the Son of God (Mt 4:3, 6).*

3. Satan tempts God's servant to please people instead of obeying God. *Satan tempted Jesus to become the political and warring Messiah that the Jewish nation was expecting. The Jews were waiting for a fighting warrior king who would expel the Romans and restore the throne of David.*

4. Satan uses the Bible in a distorted manner in order to deceive people. *Satan made a slight change in the words of God to deceive Eve in the garden, and he distorted God's words to deceive Jesus in the wilderness (Gen 2:16; 3:1, 4; Mt 4:6).*

5. The three episodes of Jesus' temptation are faced by all:
   - People face temptation to satisfy natural appetites outside of God's plans. *In the wilderness: Jesus suffered the temptation of the flesh, to have bread that God didn't provide. He was tempted to satisfy the appetites and desires of the physical body. He was tempted to use his own power to satisfy the physical need for food.*
   - People face the temptation to follow the standards of the world. *On the pinnacle of the Temple: Jesus suffered the temptation of the world, to have position and prestige without God; to live by the standards of the world. He was tempted to impress people, to use his abilities to gain glory for himself. He was tempted to put on a spectacular show to impress the people, to call attention to himself and gain prestige for himself.*
   - People face the temptation to serve Satan when they are willing to do whatever it takes to gain prestige, power and possessions. *On the high mountain: Jesus suffered the temptation to serve Satan, to have power without God. This was the temptation to do anything necessary to gain power, to be able to force others to obey and serve his every desire.*

6. Jesus is able to help people who are being tempted, and he has compassion toward them in their weakness. *Since Jesus was tempted as a man, he is able to help those who are being tempted (Hb 2:18) and to have compassion toward them in their weakness (Hb 4:15). Because Jesus was a man, he experienced hunger like any other. He did not win over temptation with divine power, but with resources available to every person.*

7. Jesus was tempted the same as every human being, but he did not yield. He remained without sin (Hb 4:15). *Eve was*

tempted in the Garden of Eden in the presence of abundance and she yielded. Jesus was tempted in the wilderness, experiencing hunger and resisted. Jesus resisted stronger temptations than any other person.

8. Temptation may be resisted with two resources: the Holy Spirit and God's Word used correctly. *Jesus used these two resources available to anyone: the Holy Spirit and the word of God.*
   - *At his baptism, the Holy Spirit descended upon Jesus (Mt 3:16). The Holy Spirit led Jesus into the wilderness (Lk 4:1) and accompanied him throughout his battle with Satan (Mt 4:1). The Holy Spirit was with Jesus until the end of his battle (Lk 4:14).*
   - *In each of the three episodes of his temptation, Jesus used the armor of the word of God by answering Satan with words from the Bible (Mt 4:4, 7, 10).*

*****

EXAMPLE # 2: Analysis of a Story Found in Multiple Texts

STORY: Four Fishermen Follow Jesus

TEXT: Matthew 4:18-22; Mark 1:16-20; Luke 5:1-11; John 1: 29-45

STRUCTURE:

Key-persons:
- Jesus, Peter

Key-location:
- Jordan River, Lake Galilee

Key-repetitions:
- Fishing/casting nets (Mt 4:18; Lk 5:4, 5, 6, 9, 10)
- Fishermen (Mt 4:18, 19; Lk 5:2, 11)
- Nets (Mt 4:18, 20, 21; Lk 5:2, 4, 5, 6)
- Boat (Mt 4:21, 22; Lk 5:2, 3 (2x), 7 (2x), 11)
- Sin (Jn 1:19; Lk 5:8)

Key-attitudes:
- Admiration of John the Baptist for Jesus
- Curiosity of Andrew and Philip wanting to get to know Jesus
- Excitement of Andrew when he told his brother Simon about Jesus
- Confidence of Jesus when he told Simon he would be called Peter; when he taught the people; when he ordered Simon to let his nets out for a catch; and when he invited the fishermen to follow him
- Reluctance of Peter to let his net out after not catching any fish all night
- Peter's fear of Jesus after catching the large number of fish
- Astonishment of the fishermen at the large number of fish caught
- Trust of the fishermen in Jesus when they left their nets and boats to follow Jesus

Initial-situation:
When Jesus began the first year of his ministry, he was unknown outside of his home town of Nazareth. John the Baptist was famous. Crowds were going to hear John and to be baptized by him.

Jesus began his public ministry at the Jordan River when he was baptized by John. In the desert, Jesus resisted temptations from Satan. After his temptations, Jesus returned to where John was baptizing.

Initial-problem:
Jesus was walking alone when John the Baptist told his followers, "Look, the Lamb of God who takes away the sin of the world! This is the one I was talking about, `A man will come after me, but he is greater than me because he was living before me.'"

Sequence of events:
BACK-STORY: John the Baptist's Followers Begin to Experience Jesus
- John the Baptist told his followers about Jesus (Jn 1:29-34).
- Andrew and Philip spent the rest of the day with him (Jn 1:35-39).

- Andrew brought his brother Simon to Jesus; Philip brought Nathanael to Jesus (Jn 1: 40-51).
- The four men made some trips with Jesus (Jn 2 - 5).
- Jesus moved from the town of Nazareth to Capernaum, a city in Galilee.

Four Fishermen Invited to Follow Jesus (Mt 4:18-22; Mk 1:16-20; Lk 5:1-11)
- Jesus walked beside Lake Galilee and saw two fishermen, the brothers Simon Peter and Andrew, casting a net (Mt 4:18).
- Jesus got into Simon Peter's boat and taught the people from the boat (Lk 5:1-3).
- Jesus told Simon Peter to let his nets out. Peter reluctantly obeyed and caught a large number of fish (Lk 5:4-7).
- Simon Peter told Jesus he was a sinful man (Lk 5:8).
- The fishermen were astonished (Lk 5:9-10).
- Jesus told Peter not to fear, from now on he would be a fisher of men (Lk 5:11).
- Jesus invited Peter and Andrew to follow him and they did (Mt 4:19-20).
- Jesus invited the brothers James and John to follow him. They left their boat, their father and their hired servants to follow Jesus (Mt 4:20-22; Mk 1:20).

Final-situation:
Four fishermen left their nets and boats to follow Jesus.

LIFE-LESSONS DISCOVERED IN THE STORY

1. A person proves that he is a disciple of Christ by following him and doing his will. *Jesus invited the four fishermen to follow him and they left their nets and boats and followed Jesus (Mt 4:18-22).*
2. To follow Jesus requires leaving something behind. *Peter and Andrew left their nets to follow Jesus (Mt 4:18-22). James and John left their boat, their father, and their hired servants to follow Jesus (Mt 4:20-22; Mk 1:20).*
3. Jesus' followers obey his orders, even if they don't agree with them. *Jesus told Simon Peter to let his nets out. Peter*

was a fisherman by trade; Jesus was a carpenter by trade. Peter thought it was the wrong time of day to fish. Peter reluctantly obeyed and was rewarded with a large catch of fish (Lk 5:4-7).
4. Only when the person recognizes that he is a sinner, unworthy of divine favors, does he become someone who is useful in the Kingdom of God. *Simon Peter told Jesus he was a sinful man (Lk 5:8). Jesus told Peter not to fear, from now on he would be a fisher men (Lk 5:11).*
5. Jesus looks for busy people to follow him. *Peter and Andrew were busy casting their nets when Jesus invited them to follow him. James and John were busy preparing their nets when Jesus invited them to follow him (Mt 4:18-22).*
6. Jesus transforms the priorities of his followers. *The priorities of the fishermen had been to catch fish. Jesus transformed their priority to catch people for God's kingdom (Mt 4:19).*

Analyze a Story by Interlocking Facts Found in Cross-References

Cross-references may lead to a linking story or text that gives information that is vital to understanding the story being analyzed. Most published Bibles contain cross-references listed in the margins or foot of each page. The cross-references list other texts that tell the same story, express similar ideas, or use identical words. Cross-references help the student who is analyzing a story in one passage to interlock it with other tellings of the same story.

Information from cross-references linking stories can be interlocked and included in the telling of the main story. Texts are interlocked to the main story for the purpose of fitting details together to ensure better comprehension of the story. Usually the interlocking stories or facts are summarized or paraphrased. Include only essential interlocking details that will make the main story better understood.

Example # 1:
Joseph's brothers threw him into a dry well. They pulled him out of the well and sold him to slave merchants for twenty pieces of silver. The merchants took Joseph to Egypt (Genesis 37:23-28). Additional information can be interlocked into the story from two cross-references.
- Joseph was terrified and pleaded for his life. Years later Joseph's brothers were fearful for their lives, and Ruben said, "We're being punished because of what we did to our brother Joseph. We saw his distress when he pleaded with us for his life" (Genesis 42:21).
- Joseph's feet were weighted down with shackles and an iron collar was put on his neck (Psalms 105:18).

Example # 2:
The story of David's Sin with Bathsheba is found in 2 Samuel 11. Interlocking information found in 2 Samuel chapters 16 and 23 gives information about David's close relationship with Bathsheba's family.

If the story of David's Sin with Bathsheba only includes facts from the text of 2 Samuel 11, listeners could conclude that David only had casual knowledge of Bathsheba's family. But 2 Samuel chapters 16 and 23 give information that David had close relationships with Bathsheba's family. 2 Samuel chapter 23 tells about the mighty warriors in David's army and contains a list of David's Thirty Mighty Warriors. Included in the thirty are Eliam, son of Ahithophel, and Uriah. Eliam, Bathsheba's father, was one of David's Thirty Mighty Warriors (2 Sam 23:34). Ahithophel, Eliam's father and Bathsheba's grandfather, was David's chief counselor. David considered Ahithophel's advice as being the counsel of God (2 Sam 16:23). Uriah, Bathsheba's husband, was one of David's Thirty Mighty Warriors (2 Sam 23:39).

EXAMPLE # 1: Analysis of a Story Using Interlocking Cross-Reference Facts

STORY: David's Sin with Bathsheba

TEXT: 1 Samuel 11:1 - 12:15;
Cross-References –2 Samuel 16: 23; 23:34, 39

STRUCTURE:

Initial-situation (*Includes the back-story*)

King Saul became the first king of Israel. However, on two occasions King Saul disobeyed the Lord. The Lord rejected Saul as king and sent the prophet to anoint young David as king.

King Saul tried to kill David; David lived as a fugitive with Saul pursuing him.

The Philistines made war on Israel and archers wounded King Saul. Saul took his own sword and fell on it.

The tribe of Judah immediately anointed David as their king. After seven years, all twelve tribes of Israel anointed David as king.

King David's men captured Jerusalem. David became more powerful because the Lord was with him. Foreign governments made treaties with David.

King David wanted to build a temple for the Lord. The Lord said David would not build a Temple, but his son would. God promised to establish David's kingdom forever. David reigned over all Israel, doing what was just and right for all his people.

David had victory every time he and his army faced enemies in battle.

Key-persons:
- David, Bathsheba, Nathan

Key-locations:
- Jerusalem, David's Palace

Key-repetitions:
- David's Thirty Mighty Warriors: three risk their lives to fetch water for David (2 Sam 23:13-17); Bathsheba's father and husband were mighty warriors (2 Sam 11:3; 2 Sam 23:34, 39).
- David's sin: He stayed home when his soldiers went to war (2 Sam 11:1); he sent a man to identify the woman taking a bath (2 Sam 11:3); David discovered he had a close relationship with her family, yet he sent for the woman (2 Sam 11:4); he slept with her (2 Sam 11:4); he tried to deceive Uriah into believing the baby was his (2 Sam 11:6-14); he sentenced Uriah to die in war (2 Sam 11:14; 12:9); he took Bathsheba as his wife (2 Sam 11:27); he ignored the Lord's command (2 Sam 12:9); his sin made God's enemies lose all respect for him (2 Sam 12:14).
- Things God did for David: God made him king (2 Sam 12:7); he saved him from Saul (2 Sam 12:7); he gave David Saul's daughter as a wife (2 Sam 12:8); he gave David both Israel and Judah to rule (2 Sam 12:8).
- David's punishment for his sins: Murder will plague David's family (2 Sam 12:10); David's family would bring him calamity (2 Sam 12:11); David's wives would sleep with someone else in broad daylight (2 Sam 12:11-12); the son born to David and Bathsheba would die (2 Sam 12:14).

Key-attitudes:
- David's laziness: he didn't go to war with his men; he napped during the day
- David's lust for Bathsheba
- David's betrayal of close friends

- David's deceiving Uriah
- Uriah's faithfulness as a soldier
- Nathan's bravery
- David's remorse when he confessed his sin
- Nathan's and the Lord's sternness when dealing with David's sin

Initial-problem:
David stayed home when his army went to war.

Sequence of events:
- David was thirsty; three of his mighty warriors risked their lives to fetch him water (2 Sam 23:13-17 – *Interlocking cross-reference*).
- David dispatched his fighting men to war, but he stayed in Jerusalem (2 Sam 11:1).
- David committed adultery with Bathsheba and she became pregnant (2 Sam 11:2-5).
- Eliam, Bathsheba's father, was one of David's Thirty Mighty Warriors (2 Sam 23:34 – *Interlocking cross-reference*).
- Uriah, Bathsheba's husband, was one of David's Thirty Mighty Warriors (2 Sam 23:39 – *Interlocking cross-reference*).
- Ahithophel, David's chief counselor, was Bathsheba's grandfather (2 Sam 16:23 – *Interlocking cross-reference*).
- David ordered Joab to let Uriah, Bathsheba's husband, be killed in battle. Then David took Bathsheba as his wife (2 Sam 11:6-27).
- The Lord sent Nathan to confront David. Nathan told David a story about a rich man who took the one and only lamb of a poor man. David exploded with anger, and Nathan told David he was the man and that he would be punished (2 Sam 12:1-12).
- David confessed his sin. Nathan replied that the Lord forgave him, but killings would never depart from his family, and the son born to David and Bathsheba would die (2 Sam 12:13-14).

Final-situation:
David's sin made the enemies of the Lord lose all respect for the Lord, and David would be punished.

Life-Lessons:

1. A first sin can entice a person to commit other sins. *David fell deeper and deeper into sin (2 Sam 11:1-17); he erred in staying home when he should have gone to war (11:1); he gave attention to a forbidden desire (2 Sam 11:3); he deliberately committed adultery (2 Sam 11:4); he tried to cover up his sin by deceiving Uriah (11:6-15); he continued the cover-up by committing murder (2 Sam 11:15, 17).*

2. Repeatedly sinning will dull a person's sensitivity to God's laws and other people's rights. *David was insensitive to the news of Uriah's death because he had become callous to his own sin (2 Sam 11:23-25).*

3. God hates sin and punishes the sinner. *David suffered the consequences of his sins (2 Sam 12:10-12).*

4. Sin: so easy the act, so painful the result. *It was so easy for David to go to bed with Bathsheba (2 Sam 11:4); however, the results were painfully long lasting (2 Sam 12:9-14). The consequences of David's sin were irreversible.*

5. Doing wrong against another person is sin against God. *David betrayed two of his Mighty Warriors: Eliam, Bathsheba's father (2 Sam 23:34) and Uriah, Bathsheba's husband (2 Sam 23:39). He also betrayed his chief counselor, Ahithophel, who was Bathsheba's grandfather (2 Sam 16:23).*

6. Actions which a person strongly condemns in another person may indicate his own character flaws. *David burned with anger when he heard the story of the rich man who took the poor man's lamb, not realizing that in condemning the rich man, he was condemning himself (2 Sam 11:6-6).*

7. A woman with a beautiful body may exploit sex in order to achieve rewards. However, such a woman is a curse and not a blessing. Whoever enjoys sexual pleasure with her is harmed and sows seeds of moral rottenness. *Bathsheba*

used her body to achieve rewards: she became queen and later queen mother. Those who loved her were harmed: her husband was betrayed and murdered. David committed adultery with her and was punished.

8. God's spokesperson must be submissive to God in order to: receive God's message, know who should receive it, give the message to the person who God targets to receive it, have courage to denounce sin, and have mercy to proclaim divine pardon. *Nathan is an example of God's spokesperson who was submissive to God. Nathan received God's message for King David (2 Sam 7:5-7); gave the message to David (2 Sam 7:8-17); had courage to denounce King David's sin (2 Sam 12:1-12); had mercy to proclaim divine pardon (2 Sam 12:13).*

9. A spiritual leader's sin causes people to lose respect for God (2 Sam 14). *David's sin caused the Lord's enemies to show contempt for the Lord.*

10. Confessed sin is forgiven; however, its consequences will endure. The person who sows his wild oats and, at the time of harvest, prays for a crop failure will have his prayer denied by God. *David confessed his sin and was forgiven; however, he suffered the consequences of his sin* (2 Sam 12:10-14).

11. Repentance is evident when the guilty person takes the responsibility for his wrong actions. *David confessed: "I have sinned against the Lord"* (2 Sam 12:13; 24:10, 17).

Editing Is Needed When Crafting a Story for Telling

When the grandchildren come to our home, my wife uses her crafting ability. For breakfast, she prepares a pancake man for her grandson and pancake girls for her granddaughters. The adults get common round pancakes made from the same dough. During the day, my wife invites her granddaughters to help her bake cookies. They craft the dough so we eat star shaped cookies, cookies with little strips of chocolate added to shape a smiley face and other cookies with chocolate added to shape a sad face. Grandmother and granddaughters craft all kinds of designs for cookies.

My wife Doris takes pride in crafting food to make it attractive. As a result, she often receives compliments on the looks as well as the taste of her cooking.

Bible translators work to accurately interpret original manuscripts into modern languages. However, translators use literate wording, expecting the Bible to be read. The storyteller needs to craft the literate story, refining it so the story can be clearly understood by listeners, yet remain biblically accurate.

The storyteller needs to craft his story for telling. He should never think that because he is familiar with a story, he doesn't need to prepare. The storyteller who does not prepare to tell a story prepares to fail.

Few Bible storytellers emphasize word for word reproduction of the text from a particular Bible translation. Most craft the story for telling.

A lady named Debbie worked in different hospitals for about thirty years. She started out as an admissions clerk. She was the first person a new patient dealt with upon entering the hospital. Debbie took down the patient's personal and medical information. Debbie moved up the promotional ladder until she became Admissions Director– responsible for managing and supervising the Admissions staff.

Debbie was single, and whenever a married employee needed time off, the hospital asked Debbie to fill in. Debbie loved her job; however, she didn't like being constantly called in to work on her days off. If she stayed home when on vacation, the hospital called, asking Debbie to come to work.

Debbie read in her church's bulletin that the church needed a Church Administrative Assistant. Debbie applied for the job and was hired.

The senior pastor emphasized to Debbie, "It's important for church staff to know when members are hospitalized. If someone phones the church to report a church member has been hospitalized, immediately send a short e-mail to all staff members' cell phones. Include essential information such as name, reason for hospitalization, and name of hospital."

The second day Debbie was on her job at the church, she sent the following e-mail to all staff members, "Sally Peterson – SOB – Mercy Hospital."

An hour after Debbie sent the e-mail, the senior pastor and assistant pastor stormed into Debbie's office. The senior pastor asked, "Debbie, what is wrong with you?"

Debbie answered, "Nothing is wrong. Why do you ask?"

The pastor answered, "You said Mrs. Sally Peterson is S O B."

Debbie asked, "Do you know what S O B means?"

The pastor answered, "Yes. S O B is a vulgar acronym for a disgusting person. It's a vulgar expression that should never be used by any staff person of this church!"

Debbie gave the sport's time out hand signal and said, "Time out! Do you know what S O B means as a medical acronym?"

The pastor answered, "No. What does it mean?"

Debbie answered, "S O B is the medical acronym for Shortness of Breath."

The pastor was confused when Debbie used a medical phrase that he didn't use in his everyday life. Listeners often become confused when preachers use biblical or church words and phrases that they don't use in their everyday lives. The storytelling-preacher needs to make adaptations in the wording of a Bible story so that it can be clearly understood by listeners, yet remain biblically accurate.

OBSERVATION: Verbatim memorization is recommended to storytellers who tell Bible stories to a group of Muslims who emphasize verbatim memorization of the Quran. Some Muslims accuse Christians of altering God's Word. If you do storytelling to Muslim groups who give emphasis to memorizing the Quran, it is wise to memorize the Bible story verbatim or to read the story. Muslims are accustomed to their teachers reciting the Quran verbatim.

BIBLICAL ACCURACY – LEVELS OF RELIABILITY

1st **Provable**: A fact or event that can be proven as true or real. A fact discovered in the Bible or from reliable historical documents.
- The daughter of Herodias by her first husband, Herod Philip, danced before King Herod Antipas and secured, at her mother's instigation, the death of John the Baptist (Matthew 14:6-8; Mark 6:21-26).
- Salome was the name of Herodias' daughter. The Gospels don't mention the girl's name, but the Jewish historian, Josephus, gives her name and information about her (Josephus Ant. 18.5.4).

2nd **Probable**: Facts that are apparently true. A reasonably intelligent and prudent person could believe the facts to be true; however, the facts can't be proved from the Bible or history. Many traditional beliefs are only probable.
- Salome wore revealing clothes when she danced before Herod, and Herod was drunk when he promised Salome anything she wanted (Matthew 14:6-8; Mark 6:21-26).

3rd **Possible**: Could be true; but no way to prove it true; neither is there a way to prove it false.
- A folk religious legend says that Salome died when passing over a frozen lake. The ice broke and Salome fell up to her neck in water. Ice fragments were violently shaken by Salome's fall. Two ice fragments crashed together and severed Salome's head from her body.

Salome had requested King Herod, her step-father, to behead John the Baptist, and she was also beheaded.
- When the flood waters began to rise, many of Noah's neighbors were saying, "That old man might not have been a fool; maybe he knew what he was talking about."

4th **Embellished**: An attempt to make a story more intriguing by using the imagination to invent details and enhance events that are not mentioned in the Bible.
- Herod's birthday was a day when the country's leaders came to the palace to celebrate. Herodias told her daughter, Salome, "This is the day I've been waiting for to shut up John the Baptist. But, I need your help. Put on revealing clothes, slip into the banquet room and do a strip tease. When Herod asks you what you want, ask for John the Baptist's head. I'll make John the Baptist pay for calling me an adulteress."
- Martha went to the street market to buy vegetables and ran into Jesus. Martha invited Jesus to stop by her house, and Jesus replied, "I'll be there in an hour, and I'll bring the boys."

The Bible expository storyteller sticks to the **provable** level of reliability. The storyteller who drops to other levels may unintentionally mislead his listeners.

The storyteller needs to prepare by organizing the Bible story for telling. Bible translators work to accurately interpret original manuscripts into modern languages, expecting the Bible to be read. The storyteller needs to craft the verbatim wording from a Bible translation into an oral story for telling.

Storytelling is an art. Each Bible storyteller needs to be faithful to the Bible and to storytelling principles when crafting a story to tell; however, particular words, sentence structure, and emphasis will vary from storyteller to storyteller.

1. Principles to follow when crafting a Bible story

Just as Bible translators edit the Bible so it is easy to read, Bible storytellers need to edit Bible stories for telling. The crafted story should be accurate in order to preserve the integrity of the

Bible story. Some principles need to be followed in editing a Bible story for telling:

- <u>Stay as close to the verbatim words found in your translation as an oral narrative will allow</u>. However, when biblical wording will not be understood by listeners, use simplified words or phrases that listeners will understand.

- <u>When editing, always stay true to biblical facts</u>. Be faithful to the meaning of the original text that tells the Bible story.

- <u>Craft the story so listeners understand the story in the same way the original hearers did</u>. Editing is often needed for listeners to understand the Bible story in the same way as the original listeners/readers understood it.
  - Use terms and phrases that your listeners use in normal conversation. Biblical words not used by listeners need to be edited and changed into words listeners use in normal conversation.
    Example # 1: Most listeners would not understand the phrase, "Adam knew his wife" (Gen 4:1). They would understand something similar to, "Adam slept with his wife."
    Example # 2: Uriah's words to David, "The ark and Israel and Judah are staying in tents, and my commander Joab and my lord's men are camped in the open country. How could I go to my house to eat and drink and make love to my wife? As surely as you live, I will not do such a thing!" (2 Samuel 11:11 NIV). These sentences could be edited to say, "My commander-in-chief and fellow soldiers are camped out in the open country. My duties as an officer during a time of war prevent me from going home to make love with my wife."
  - Change unfamiliar biblical words to words or phrases listeners can understand.
    Examples: Change "publican" to "tax collector who worked for a foreign occupying government"; change John the Baptist's reference to "sons of Abraham" to "descendants of Abraham"; change the biblical word "Pharisee" to "respected conservative religious lay

leader"; change "Sadducee" to "liberal upper class priest"; change "scribe" to "scholar of Scripture."

2. Suggestions for crafting a Bible story for telling

1st <u>Replace most pronouns with proper names</u>. Bible translators avoided redundance in stories by using pronouns. Literate readers know who is speaking to whom or who is acting and what he is doing. But oral listeners can become confused about who is speaking or who is doing what. Resolve this by replacing pronouns with proper names. Reading the crafted story where pronouns were replaced by proper names seems redundant, but it is helpful to oral listeners.

2nd <u>Compound proper names with their title or roles</u>. This helps listeners know who the storyteller is talking about. Repeat the compounded title/role-proper name several times in the story.
Example:
Names can be compounded with title or role in the story of Naaman's healing from 2 Kings 5: commander Naaman; Israelite servant girl; prophet Elisha; Elisha's servant, Gehazi. This looks redundant when reading, but is most helpful to oral listeners.

3rd <u>Proper names of minor characters may be replaced with their title or role</u>. Instead of using the name, give the title such as: king, prophet, military commander, son, etc.
Examples:
- When telling David's story, most of the time Joab's name can be replaced with his title of commander-in-chief of David's army.
- Ben-Hadad, king of Aram, was an enemy of King Ahab of Israel (1 Ki 20:1-34). The proper name, Ben-Hadad could be replaced by "King of Israel's enemy."

4th <u>Focus on key-characters and key-events in the story</u>.
- It is not necessary to include unfamiliar details, minor characters' names, proper names of geographical locations and/or people group names in many stories. In

fact, including all details may overload listeners with details they cannot understand.
- Many oral storytellers try not to use more than three proper names in a given story, unless other names are already known from previous stories.

5th   <u>Precede dialog with the name of the speaker and the one being addressed</u>. State the speaker's proper name and the proper name of the person being addressed. Quotations should not be interrupted by speaker identification. Neither should the speaker be identified at the end of a dialogue. Some stories, that are recorded in the Bible, interrupt a dialogue to identify who is speaking, or the speaker is identified at the end of a quotation.

Examples found in the story of Lazarus' resurrection:
- "Lord," Martha said to Jesus, "if you had been here, my brother would not have died" (John 11:21 NIV).
  Change to: Martha said to Jesus, "Lord, if you had been here, my brother Lazarus wouldn't have died."
- "Where have you laid him?" he asked. "Come and see, Lord," they replied (John 11:34 NIV).
  Change to: Jesus asked, "Where did you lay him?" Mary and the Jews replied, "Lord, come and see."
- "Take away the stone," he said (John 11:39 NIV).
  Change to: Jesus said, "Take away the stone."

6th   <u>Keep sentences short and uncomplicated</u>. Break longer sentences into shorter ones. Subordinate clauses (dependent clauses) are difficult to follow by listeners and need to be changed into short sentences.

Example:
- "As Jesus and his disciples were on their way, he came to a village where a woman named Martha opened her home to him" (Lk 10:38 NIV).
  I would edit this verse for telling and say, "Jesus and his disciples were traveling to Jerusalem. Jesus came to a village, and a woman named Martha opened her home to him."

7th   Brief explanation may be included in the story about facts or customs not understood by listeners. Facts that original listeners understood may leave today's audience confused. This presents the need for the storyteller to include information not found in the story to make the story understood by today's listeners. The storyteller may remain true to the biblical narrative and include complementary facts to enable his listeners to clearly understand the Bible story.
Examples:
- The first listeners to the narrative of Jesus' birth would understand that an engaged Jewish couple had a legal commitment that could only be terminated by divorce. The engaged couple was called husband and wife even though the marriage ceremony that initiated the couple living together would happen in a distant future. Today such a couple would be called engaged.
- Those who heard Jesus tell the Parable of the Pharisee and the Publican who went to the Temple to pray (Luke 18:9-14), understood who Pharisees and Publicans were. It would be helpful to include the complementary facts that Pharisees were respected spiritual leaders who were legalistic in following religious traditions of their ancestors. Publicans were corrupt Jewish tax collectors who worked for the occupying Roman government. Tax collectors became wealthy by overcharging their fellow citizens. Publicans were despised and called traitors by fellow Jews.

The Bible storyteller should not exaggerate and invent facts not found in the biblical narrative, but he may need to include brief explanations that clarify the story for today's listeners. It may be helpful to include interlocking facts discovered in other texts.

8th   In some stories, it is wise to avoid details that contain events that are inflammatory or socially unacceptable to listeners' cultural worldview. It is wise to skip details that are so foreign to listeners' cultural or worldview that listeners would focus on the violation of their cultural or worldview and not hear the story.

Examples:
- A tribal leader in the Amazon region of Brazil told a missionary, "Jesus wrong! Wise man no build house on rock. Everybody know: you sleep on rock, you wake with backache. Builder drive poles through sand, not rock, to make house."
- Some macho cultures believe that if a man and woman are alone, the man shows his manhood by making sexual advances. The story of Jesus being alone with the Samaritan woman in John 4 presents a problem to macho cultures. It could be wise to leave out details of the disciples' departure to buy food.
- A Bible storyteller in Africa told the story where Jesus said, "I am the Good Shepherd" (John 10). Listeners asked, "What was wrong with Jesus? Only crazies or drunks are shepherds!"
- The story of Deborah and Barak (Judges 4) ends with the enemy warrior Sisera fleeing to the tent of Jael, the wife of Heber. Heber's family and Sisera's king were friends. The woman Jael offered hospitality, warrior Sisera went to sleep and the woman Jael killed warrior Sisera as he slept. Middle Eastern cultures are shocked at the way this ending breaks their cultural values, because (1) anyone who is under your roof is under your protection, and (2) a man never ever enters the quarters of a woman who is not his wife.

9th In some stories, it is wise to avoid using words or terms that present a problem to listeners. Some terms are inflammatory to certain listeners. Different words that have the same meaning can be confusing.

Examples:
- The man Abram had his name changed to Abraham. This may confuse listeners. It may be better to call him Abraham from the beginning, but mention that he had been called Abram, that God changed his name, and explain the difference in meaning of both names.
- Bible stories use the words "Hebrew," "Israel," "Israelite," "Ephram," and "Jew," referring to the same people. Sometimes, more than two of the above words are used in the same story. It would be less confusing, for the

listeners, to exchange those words with the phrase, "descendant of Abraham."
- The term, "Israelite," presents a problem to some Muslim listeners. It could be better to substitute the term with the phrase, "descendant of Abraham."
- Some stories contain more than one word when referring to God. If listeners worship multiple gods, they may think that different words for God are actually referring to different gods. If the storyteller always uses the same word when referring to God, he would avoid confusion.

10th   <u>Condense longer Bible stories for telling</u>. Some stories are very long and need to be shortened for telling. These stories can be edited and condensed by dropping out details that load the story but are unnecessary to understand the main story-line. Many stories contain names of people and places that were relevant to the original listeners, but are irrelevant to listeners today. Nonessential events to the main story-line can be edited out making the condensed story clearly understood.

Examples:
- Stories of Abraham, Joseph, Moses, David, Birth of Jesus, Week of Jesus' Crucifixion, and Appearances of Jesus After His Resurrection are too long to tell verbatim. A compact narrative can be crafted that edits out some minor events and has bridge-sentences that connect the main parts. The listeners can understand the story-line without struggling to understand the relevance of details that aren't essential to the story-line.
- The proper names of unfamiliar geographic locations and minor characters can be edited out. The story of King Saul's disobeying God by offering a sacrifice when only priests were authorized to officiate a public sacrifice is found in 1 Samuel 13. People who have no knowledge of Palestine would be confused by the different geographic locations mentioned. The story would be better understood if the names of geographic locations were edited out.
- The story of Jesus' birth does not suffer when the genealogies of Jesus are edited out.

11th   <u>A story that is told in several books of the Bible may be harmonized into one story</u>. By comparing a story retold in different books, it is possible to acquire more details about the same event.

3. Pay special attention to dialogue, conflict, contrast, and divine intervention found in the Bible text

While crafting the story for telling, pay special attention to dialogue, conflict, contrast and divine intervention found in the Bible text that tells the story. The Bible uses dialogue for emphasis. Conflict is the spice of every story.

Contrast often reveals evidence about character and choices. Jacob and Esau serve as contrasts to one another. In some stories, two people, who are similar, serve to contrast one another. Jacob and his father-in-law, Laban, were both manipulators and serve as a contrast to one another. The attitude of God toward Nineveh is viewed in contrast with Jonah's attitude.

Build a character through action and dialogues, not through description.

Stories are character-driven. Characters act, experience conflict and undertake the struggles in a story. The events in the story are generated by the key-character's predicaments. The storyteller must make his story-listeners see, hear, feel and know the key-character(s).

Most Bible stories gravitate toward dialogue. Dialogue is the lifeblood of many Bible stories. Large portions of most stories are carried by dialogue. Often, the text renders an important event mainly through dialogue. Transaction between key-characters typically unfolds through dialogues with minimal interpretation of the narrator. Dialogue can include internal dialogue, where a character talks to himself. Characters' feelings and emotions of love, hatred, anger, compassion, etc. are presented through dialogue and actions, not description.

The Bible gives importance to dialogue and the story-crafter should emphasize dialogue. Show characters' emotions through action and dialogue. Bible stories present characters through action and dialogues, not through description. The storyteller should show, not tell. Instead of using abstract descriptive words, he should use concrete descriptive words. Instead of saying: "Jacob was a man without moral standards," show this characteristic by description of actions or dialogue. It would be better to say: "Jacob lied to his father in order to steal his brother's inheritance."

Example: the text in Genesis 4 says that Cain was very angry. Then it uses:
- Description: Cain's face was dark with rage.
- Dialogue: God asked Cain, "Why are you angry? Why is your face dark with rage?"
- Action: Cain attacked his brother Abel and killed him.

4. Be accurate to the biblical narrative

Be accurate. Stay true to facts mentioned in the Bible. Bible stories are structured for teaching and retention. Bible storytellers do not have the freedom to dress up and change the story. The expository Bible storyteller should be true to the facts in the Bible text. He does not have the freedom to embellish the story. He should not exaggerate and recreate the story – inventing facts, situations and events not found in the biblical narrative. He should be exact in order not to mislead.

Example of what not to do:
Do not embellish the story of the flood found in Genesis 6-9 by saying, "After two days of raining, flood waters began to rise. Noah's neighbors said to one another, 'Maybe the old man knew what he was talking about.' After four days of rain, Noah's neighbors climbed onto tree trunks or anything that would float. They paddled to the ark and pounded on the door, shouting, 'Noah, it's your neighbor; open the door; let us in!'"

5. Avoid interpretation during the crafting of a story

Do not interrupt a story with explanation. Do not add a moral to the end of the story. Leave the teaching or preaching until after the story has been completely told. Many preachers want to preach or teach a story rather than tell it. They keep interrupting the story to interpret or make comments. They must make a conscious effort to make a paradigm shift and change former habits in order to become a storyteller.

Many preachers treat a Bible story the same way as I treated a common story often told to children.

THE LITTLE RED HEN INTERPRETED
Example of what not to do:

Little Red Hen was in the barnyard searching for food. The hen is the female member of the chicken family. The chicken (*Gallus gallus domesticus*) is a domesticated fowl, a subspecies of the Red Jungle Fowl. The chicken is the most common domestic animal. Humans keep chickens primarily as a source of food, consuming both their meat and their eggs. Chickens are omnivores. In the wild, they often scratch at the soil to search for seeds, insects and even larger animals such as lizards, small snakes, or young mice.

The Little Red Hen found some grains of wheat. Wheat is a type of grass grown all over the world for its highly nutritious and useful grain. It is one of the top three most produced crops in the world, along with corn and rice. Wheat is a grass that grows between two and four feet tall. The wheat plant has a long stalk that terminates in a tightly formed cluster of plump kernels enclosed by a beard of bristly spikes.

The Little Red Hen asked her feathered friends, "Cluck, cluck. Who will help me plant this wheat?"
Goose said, "Honk, honk, not I."
The term goose applies to the female in the geese family. The male is called a gander.

Duck said, "Quack, quack, not I."

The word "duck" comes from Old English. It is a derivative of the verb dūcan meaning to duck, bend down low to get under something or dive. The word "duck" refers to the adult female. The adult male is called a "drake."

Little Red Hen said, "Cluck, cluck. I'll plant it by myself." And she planted the grains of wheat. Planting involves breaking the soil. The soil may be ploughed or it may be broken with a hoe and a rake. Then wheat seed is put about an inch deep into the soil.

The wheat grew. It became ripe and was ready for harvest. Wheat is ready for harvest when the heads of the grain start to bend the stalks with the weight of the kernels. This, in combination with the golden color, indicates that it is time to harvest the wheat.

Little Red Hen asked her feathered friends, "Cluck, cluck. Who'll help me harvest this wheat?"
Goose said, "Honk, honk, not I."
Duck said, "Quack, quack, not I."
Little Red Hen said, "Cluck, cluck. Then I'll harvest it by myself." And she harvested the wheat.

After the wheat was harvested, Little Red Hen asked her feathered friends, "Cluck, cluck. Who'll help me take this wheat to the mill?"
When threshed, wheat ear breaks up into spikelets. To obtain the grain, further processing, such as milling or pounding, is needed to remove the hulls or husks. On threshing, the chaff breaks up, releasing the grains.

Goose said, "Honk, honk, not I."
Duck said, "Quack, quack, not I."
Little Red Hen said, "Cluck, cluck. Then I'll take it by myself." And she took the wheat to the mill.

Little Red Hen brought flour home from the mill. Then she asked her feathered friends, "Cluck, cluck. Who'll help me bake some bread with this flour?"

Baking is the technique of prolonged cooking of flower mixed with other ingredients by dry heat, normally in an oven, but also in hot ashes or on hot stones. Baking is primarily used for the preparation of bread.

Goose said, "Honk, honk, not I."
Duck said, "Quack, quack, not I."
Little Red Hen said, "Cluck, cluck. Then I'll bake the bread by myself." And she baked the bread.

Little Red asked her feathered friends, "Cluck, cluck. Who'll help me eat this bread?"
Goose said, "Honk, honk, I will!"
Duck said, "Quack, quack, I will!"
Little Red Hen said, "Cluck, cluck. No you won't; I'll eat it by myself!"

6. Structure the crafted story with the initial-situation, the sequence of events and the final-situation

- Establish the initial-situation from information found in the context or the back-story.

    Begin crafting the story with the initial-situation which gives basic information that the listeners need to know to understand the story. This information is usually found in the context preceding the story-text. If needed, include additional information that will help the listeners:
    - Include bridging information from previously told stories. A bridging example is found in the Bible. Genesis ends with Joseph's story, which explains how Abraham's descendants came to live in Egypt. Exodus begins with bridging information that a new king, who did not know about Joseph, came to power (Exodus 1:8).
    - If needed, include the back-story as part of the initial-situation. Most stories stand alone with just the information found in the context immediately preceding the text of the story, but some stories need the back-story to be fully understood.

- Follow the structural order of the biblical narrative utilizing the sequence of events in chronological order, the historical sequence in which the events occurred.

  After crafting the initial-situation, follow the structural order of the story, utilizing the sequence of events in chronological order.

  Include dialogue and actions. Bible stories seldom describe the moral-character or description of people. Instead, moral-character is revealed through other means – such as dialogue, actions, or choices made.

- End the story with the final situation.

7. The crafted story may include bullet points listing the sequence of events, or it may be written out in full

Most storytellers do not need to write out the story word for word. Some do. The main reason for writing out the Bible story word for word is to be able to share the story with people who would never go to the effort of analyzing and crafting a story for themselves. Many people are willing to tell a Bible story that someone else crafted for telling; however, they would never tell it if they had to study the Bible story and craft it for telling.

EXAMPLES OF STORIES CRAFTED FOR TELLING

These stories were analyzed in the previous chapter.

EXAMPLE # 1: Cain and Abel (Genesis 4:1-16)

God placed Adam and Eve in the Garden of Eden and forbade them to eat fruit from the tree that was in the center of the garden. Adam and Eve disobeyed God's order and ate the forbidden fruit. God expelled Adam and Eve from the Garden of Eden.

Adam slept with his wife Eve. Eve became pregnant and gave birth to Cain. Eve said, "The Lord helped me give birth to a man." Later she gave birth to Cain's brother Abel. Abel became a herdsman and kept flocks; Cain became a farmer and worked the soil (4:1-2).

Time passed. Brother Cain brought some produce from his farm as an offering to the Lord. But brother Abel brought choice cuts of meat from the firstborn of his flock. The Lord accepted Abel and his offering, but rejected Cain and his offering (4:3-4).

Cain became very angry; his face was dark with rage. The Lord asked Cain, "Why are you angry? Why is your face so dark with rage? If you do what is right, I'll accept you. But if you do not do what is right, sin is crouching at your door waiting to pounce; it is out to get you, but you must tame it" (4:5-7).

One day Cain invited his brother Abel, "Let's go out into the field." Cain and Abel were in the field, and Cain attacked his brother Abel and killed him (4:8). Cain murdered his brother Able because Cain's own actions were evil and his brother Able's were righteous (*Interlocking fact from* 1 John 3:12).

The Lord asked Cain, "Where is your brother Abel?"
Cain replied, "I don't know. Is it my job to take care of my brother?"
The Lord asked, "What have you done? Listen! Your brother's blood cries out to me from the ground. From now on you'll receive nothing but curses from the ground, which received your brother Able's blood whom you murdered. Cain, you'll work the ground but it will no longer yield good crops for you. You'll be a restless tramp upon the earth, a wanderer from place to place."

Cain complained to the Lord, "My punishment is too much. I can't take it! Today you're driving me from the land. I have to hide from you; I can never again face you. I'll be a homeless fugitive and a tramp wandering on the earth. Whoever finds me will kill me."

The Lord answered Cain, "Not so; if anyone kills Cain, he'll suffer vengeance seven times greater than your punishment." Then the Lord put a mark on Cain. It was a warning to anyone who met Cain not to kill him (Gen 4:8-15).

Cain went out from God's presence and lived in No-Man's-Land, east of Eden (4:16).

EXAMPLE # 2: **The Widow's Oil** (2 Kings 4:1-7)

Prophet Elijah was taken to heaven. Prophet Elisha became Elijah's successor and began his prophetic ministry. There was war in the land.

The widow of a man from the company of the prophets called out to prophet Elisha, "Your servant, my husband, is dead. You know that my husband was devoted to the Lord. But now my husband's creditor is coming to take my two boys as his slaves."
Prophet Elisha replied to the widow, "How can I help you? Tell me, what do you have in your house?"
The widow answered, "Nothing at all, except a little jar of oil."
Prophet Elisha said, "Go around and ask all your neighbors for empty containers. Don't ask for just a few. Then you and your sons go inside your house and close the door behind you. Pour oil into all the containers. When each is filled, set it aside."
The widow did what prophet Elisha said. She shut the door. Only the widow and her sons were in the house. The sons brought the containers to their mother and she poured the oil. When all the containers were full, the mother said to her sons, "Bring me another container."
One son replied, "There is no empty container left." Then the oil stopped flowing.
The widow returned to prophet Elisha and told him what happened. Elisha said, "Go, sell the oil and pay your debts. You and your sons can live on what is left" (2 Kg 4:1-7).

EXAMPLE # 3: **Jesus Calls Levi** (also called Matthew) (Luke 5:27-32)

Jesus was at the beginning of the second year of his public ministry. Jesus had performed several miracles and had called four fishermen to follow him.

Jesus went out and saw a tax collector by the name of Levi sitting at his tax booth. Levi was also called Matthew. Tax collectors were Jewish citizens who collaborated with the Roman occupying forces. Tax collectors were despised as traitors by fellow Jews. Jesus invited Levi, the tax collector, "Follow me." Levi got up, left everything and followed Jesus.

Preaching with Storytelling © Jackson Day

Then Levi gave a large banquet for Jesus at his house. A large crowd of tax collectors and others with bad reputations were Levi's guests. The respected conservative religious leaders, and the Scripture scholars complained to Jesus' disciples, "Why do you eat and drink with tax collectors and sinners?"

Jesus answered them, "Healthy people don't need a doctor. Sick people need a doctor. I didn't come to invite the righteous, but sinners to repentance" (Lk 5:27-32).

HARMONIZING DIFFERENT TELLINGS OF A STORY INTO ONE STORY

EXAMPLE: Four Fishermen Follow Jesus
(Matthew 4:18-22; Mark 1:16-20; Luke 5:1-11, John 1: 29-45)

Initial-situation *(includes the back-story)*
John the Baptist Tells His Followers About Jesus

One day, John the Baptist was with two of his disciples, Andrew and Philip. John the Baptist saw Jesus walking nearby. John the Baptist said, "Look, the Lamb of God!" The two disciples followed Jesus and spent the rest of the day with him. It was about four o'clock in the afternoon (Jn 1:29-39).

Andrew found his brother Simon Peter, and took his brother to Jesus. Philip found his friend Nathanael, and Philip brought his friend Nathanael to Jesus (Jn 1:43-51). Andrew, Simon Peter, Philip and Nathanael made several trips with Jesus during his first year of public ministry (Jn 2 - 5).

John the Baptist was imprisoned. Jesus began his second year of public ministry. Jesus moved from his home town of Nazareth to Capernaum, a city in Galilee.

Four Fishermen Invited to Follow Jesus (*Main story*)
(Mt 4:18-22; Mk 1:16-20; Lk 5:1-11)

Jesus was walking beside Lake Galilee and he saw two brothers, Simon, called Peter, and his brother Andrew. Peter and Andrew were fishermen; they were casting a net into the lake (Mt 4:18).

Jesus stood beside Lake Galilee; people crowded around Jesus listening to the word of God. Jesus noticed two boats at the shore of the lake. Jesus got into the boat belonging to Simon Peter. Jesus asked Peter to put out a little from shore. Then Jesus sat down and taught the people from the boat.

Jesus finished speaking and told fisherman Simon Peter, "Push out into deep water and let your nets out for a catch."

Simon Peter answered, "Master, we worked hard all night and haven't caught anything. But because you say so, I'll let out the nets."

The fishermen let out the nets. Immediately, they caught such a large number of fish that their nets began to break. They signaled their partners in the other boat to come and help them. The fishermen filled both boats so full that they were almost sinking.

Simon Peter fell to his knees before Jesus and said, "Get away from me, Lord; I'm a sinful man!" Peter and all his co-fishermen were astonished at the catch of fish they had taken.

Jesus told Simon Peter, "Don't be afraid; from now on you'll catch men" (Lk 5:1-11).

Jesus called Peter and his brother Andrew, "Come follow me, and I'll make you fishers of men." At once they dropped their nets and followed him.

Then Jesus went to where James and his brother John were sitting in a boat with their father Zebedee, mending their nets. Jesus called the brothers James and John. Immediately James and John left their father in the boat with the hired servants and followed Jesus (Mt 4:18-22; Mk 1:20).

BIBLE STORY USING INTERLOCKING FACTS FOUND IN CROSS-REFERENCES

EXAMPLE: David's Sin with Bathsheba
(2 Samuel 11:1 - 12:14)
(Cross-References – 2 Samuel 16: 23; 23:34, 39)

Initial-situation (*Includes the back-story*)

King Saul became the first king of Israel. However, on two occasions King Saul disobeyed the Lord, and the Lord rejected Saul as king. The Lord sent prophet Samuel to anoint young David as king. King Saul tried to kill David; David lived as a fugitive in wilderness hideouts with Saul pursuing him.

The Philistines made war on Saul's army and King Saul died in battle. The tribe of Judah immediately anointed David as their king. After seven years, all the tribes of Israel anointed David as king.

King David's men captured Jerusalem and he took up residence there. King David became more powerful because the Lord was with him. Foreign governments made treaties with King David.

King David wanted to build a temple for the Lord. The Lord told David that he wouldn't build a temple, but his son would. The Lord promised to establish David's kingdom forever. King David reigned over all Israel, doing what was just and right for all his people.

King David had victory every time he and his army faced enemies in battle.

(*Interlocking cross-reference as part of back-story*)

The following event shows the loyalty David's Mighty Warriors had for him. Once, a band of enemies surrounded David. David was thirsty and longed for water and said, "Oh, that someone would get me water from the well near the gate of Bethlehem!" Three Mighty Warriors slipped through enemy lines, drew water from the well near the gate of Bethlehem, and brought it back to David. David refused to drink the water; instead, he poured it out as a gift to the Lord. David said, "I couldn't drink this water; men risked their lives to get it!" (2 Sam 23:13-17).

Story: David's Sin with Bathsheba

It was the custom for kings to go off to war in the spring time. King David dispatched his commander-in-chief with the king's soldiers to war, but David stayed in Jerusalem (2 Sam 11:1).

After lunch one afternoon, King David took a nap. David got up from his nap and walked around on the flat roof of his palace. From the vantage point of the roof, David saw a beautiful woman bathing. David asked a man about the woman. The man reported, "She's Bathsheba, Eliam's daughter and Uriah's wife" (2 Sam 11:2-3).

King David didn't know Bathsheba; however, he knew her family. Eliam, Bathsheba's father was one of David's Thirty Mighty Warriors (2 Sam 23:34). Ahithophel, Eliam's father and Bathsheba's grandfather, was David's chief counselor. David considered that Ahithophel's counsel was the very words of God (2 Sam 16:23). Uriah, Bathsheba's husband, was also one of David's elite Thirty Mighty Warriors (2 Sam 23:39).

King David sent messengers to fetch Bathsheba. She came to him; David and Bathsheba went to bed. Bathsheba returned home. Later, Bathsheba sent word to David, "I'm pregnant" (2 Sam 11:4-5).

David sent word for his army's commander-in-chief to send warrior Uriah, Bathsheba's husband, to Jerusalem. Warrior Uriah arrived and David requested information about the war. Then David told Uriah, "Go to your house and have a good night's sleep."
Uriah left the palace, but slept on a mat at the palace entrance with David's servants. Uriah didn't go home.
The next morning, David asked Uriah, "Why didn't you go home?"
Uriah answered, "My commander-in-chief and fellow soldiers are sleeping in tents. My duties as an officer, during a time of war, kept me from going home to sleep with my wife!"
David told Uriah, "Stay here today; tomorrow I'll send you back." However, the next day, David invited Uriah to eat the evening meal with him. David got Uriah drunk. But afterwards, Uriah didn't go home, he slept on his mat at the palace entrance with David's servants (2 Sam 11:6-13).

The next morning, David wrote a letter to his commander-in-chief and sent it with Uriah. David wrote his commander-in-chief,

"Put Uriah in the front line where the fighting is most fierce. Let him be killed in battle" (2 Sam 11:14-16).

Bathsheba heard that her husband Uriah was dead. Bathsheba grieved for her husband Uriah. After the time of mourning was over, David sent for Bathsheba and she became his wife. She gave birth to David's son. But the Lord didn't like what David had done (2 Sam 11:26-27).

The Lord sent prophet Nathan to David. Prophet Nathan told David, "There were two men in the same town, one rich and the other poor. The rich man had many sheep and cattle, but the poor man had nothing except one little female lamb which he bought and raised. It grew up with the poor man's children. It shared his food, drank from his cup and even slept in his arms. The lamb was like a daughter to him. Now a traveler stopped to visit the rich man. But the rich man was too stingy to take one of his own sheep or cattle to feed the traveler. Instead, the rich man took the poor man's one lamb and cooked it for his guest to eat."

King David exploded with anger and told prophet Nathan, "The rich man who did this deserves to die! The rich man must pay for that lamb four times over, for his crime and his stinginess!"

Prophet Nathan told David, "You are the man! This is what the Lord, the God of Israel, says, `I made you king over Israel; I saved you from King Saul; I gave you King Saul's daughter and other wives; I gave you both Israel and Judah. Why did you ignore the Lord's command and do this great evil? You murdered Uriah with the sword of your enemy, and you took Uriah's wife as your wife! Now, the sword will never depart from your house; murder and killing will continually plague your family. I'm going to bring calamity upon you out of your own family. I'll take your wives and give them to one who is close to you, and he'll lie with your wives in broad daylight. You did it in secret, but I'll do it to you in broad daylight with all of Israel watching.'"

David told prophet Nathan, "I've sinned against the Lord."

Nathan replied, "The Lord forgives your sin. You're not going to die for it. Your sin made the Lord's enemies lose all respect for him; therefore, the son born to you will die" (2 Sam 12:1-14).

MEAT AND VEGETABLES OF PREACHING WITH STORYTELLING
Expository Bible Storytelling

The traditional meal for most families includes a meat and vegetables. A healthy meat and vegetable diet includes red meats, poultry, or fish, and a variety of vegetables. Meats provide proteins and iron, while vegetables contain a variety of vitamins and minerals needed for the body. A healthy meat and vegetable diet boosts the immune system and helps maintain overall health.

The meat and vegetable diet for Preaching with Storytelling would be Expository Bible Storytelling. The method includes telling the Bible story followed by expository preaching. The preacher begins by telling the Bible story; then he develops life-lessons discovered in the Bible story into preaching points.

The expository preacher limits himself to his chosen text of Scripture. His job is to make the text understood by his listeners. Every word from the pulpit amplifies, elaborates, or illustrates the text at hand. He considers Scripture his authority and limits himself to his text. His goal is for his listeners to understand the text.

The expository storytelling-preacher communicates a Bible story accurately and fully through telling the Bible story and then explaining life-lessons discovered in the story. Every word from the pulpit amplifies, elaborates, or illustrates life-lessons found in his story-text.

SUGGESTED WAYS TO PREACH BIBLE STORIES

1. **Preach Bible stories in a Chronological Bible Storytelling Track**

A **Chronological Bible Storytelling Track** begins with the creation story in Genesis; next the story of disobedience of Adam and Eve in the garden; next Cain and Abel; next Noah and the flood; continues through Old Testament stories in their historical sequence; begins New Testament stories with the announcements of the births of John the Baptist and Jesus; continues with events in the life of Jesus in historical sequence; continues through the Book of Acts; places the Epistles in their chronological order within Acts; finishes with stories related to the end times. This approach is often called "**Storying the Bible.**"

2. **Preach a series of Bible stories**

Many possibilities exist for using Bible stories in a series. *For example*:
- Principal events and characters in Genesis
- Events in the life of a key-person (for example: Abraham, David, Peter or Paul)
- Miracles in the Old Testament
- Key women in the Bible
- Single adults in the Bible
- Conflicts in the Bible
- Jesus' encounter with people who suffered discrimination
- Parables of Jesus
- Miracles of Jesus
- People who talked alone with Jesus
- People praised by Jesus
- Paul's missionary journeys
- Events in the life of the early church

3. **Preach a solitary story**

Solitary storytelling isolates a story to be presented to a specific group for a specific occasion. *For example*: on a certain Sunday, the preacher decides to use as the text for his sermon, David's sin with Bathsheba (2 Samuel 11 - 12).

4. **Preach a Bible story for a specific situation**

Take advantage of the numerous situations in which Bible Storytelling can be effective such as a funeral, a wedding, an invitation to visit the sick, a birthday party, or an anniversary celebration. Tell one or more stories that are appropriate in the situation.

For example: A church was celebrating youth who were graduating from high school. The pastor preached about young Daniel and his friends' determination to be faithful to God at the court of Nebuchanezzar (Daniel 1:1-20).

5. Preach a Bible story to deal with specific questions or needs

A Bible story can be used to resolve a specific question or spiritual need.
For example:
- A man was caught in an FBI sting when he went to a house expecting to meet and have sex with a fourteen-year old girl. A consequence of his arrest was he became a registered sex-offender. The man's shame and embarrassment led him to seek counseling from his wife's pastor. The sex-offender confessed his addiction to porn, began counseling with a Christian counselor, and confessed his sins and belief in Jesus. However, some church members did not want a registered sex-offender attending their church. The storytelling-preacher could tell the story of the prostitute who anointed Jesus' feet with perfume to show that Jesus is willing to forgive and accept sex-offenders into his kingdom (Luke 7:36-50).
- A new believer became drunk. Some church members don't believe the backslider deserves another chance. The story of Jesus' encounter with Peter after Peter's betrayal could be applied (John 21:1-23).

Worksheet: SERMON OUTLINE FOR BIBLE STORY-TEXT

Bible Story Performed Orally

Sermon Divisions, Utilizing the Preaching Cycle

1. 1st Sermon Division (1st Life-lesson chosen from story-text to be preached)
   Explanation:

   Illustration:

   Application:

2. 2nd Sermon Division (2nd Life-lesson chosen from story-text to be preached)
   Explanation:

   Illustration:

   Application:

3. 3rd Sermon Division (3rd Life-lesson chosen from story-text to be preached)
   Explanation:

   Illustration:

   Application:

CONCLUSION
   1st Summarize:
   - Principal facts of Bible story
   - Life-lessons (divisions of the sermon) treated

   2nd Invite listeners to change by putting truths and applications presented into action

SERMON OUTLINE

1. The Bible Story Performed Orally

The storytelling-preacher starts his sermon by performing the Bible story that is his text. The only introduction needed is something similar to:
- I'm going to tell you a story found in the Bible, Exodus, chapters 1 - 4.
- I'm going to tell you an old, old story, but it is a true story found in the Bible.

After the sentence introduction, perform the story, utilizing the sequence of events in chronological order. Start with the initial-situation (background), continue with the sequence of events and end with the final-situation.

This approach requires a paradigm shift for preachers accustomed to literate-linear preaching where ideas reign. They were trained to emphasize the logic of persuasion using the path of reason. They are accustomed to seeing the task of preaching as analyzing the ideas of a text. Texts that are story in nature are analyzed to find their ideas. When narrating a story, these preachers interrupt the story to call attention to an idea discovered in the story. These preachers need a paradigm shift, so they will perform the story with the goal that listeners experience the story. The storytelling-preacher wants his listeners to identify with how they are similar or different to key-characters in the story, and identify with how God works in their lives similar to the way he worked in the lives of the key-characters.

2. Sermon Divisions, Utilizing the Preaching Cycle

The expository storytelling-preacher communicates a Bible story accurately and fully through performing the entire Bible story and then afterwards he elaborates on life-lessons discovered in the story. Every spoken word from the pulpit amplifies, elaborates, or illustrates life-lessons discovered in the story.

SELECTING LIFE-LESSONS TO BECOME SERMON DIVISIONS

The storytelling-preacher must select from his Bible story life-lessons to become sermon divisions. When the preacher analyzes the Bible story, he may discover ten, twenty, thirty or more life-lessons. It would be unwise for him to present all life-lessons discovered in one sermon. He must choose the life-lessons that best meet the needs of his listeners.

Choosing life-lessons from a Bible story to preach can be compared to the man who is building a house and has a Ford F-150 pick-up to transport building material. He goes to the building supply store that has everything needed to build his house. However, he cannot take all the wood, cement, brick, plumbing pipes, electrical wiring, Sheetrock, and roofing material in one trip. He must determine the material he most needs to do the task at hand. The builder with the pick-up who tries to take too much building material in one trip will damage the body of his truck and overheat the engine.

The storytelling-preacher has a limited amount of time and can't present all the life-lessons he finds in a single Bible story in one sermon. Listeners can only take in a limited amount of information in one session. Less is better. The storytelling-preacher must select life-lessons that are most needed for his listeners in their present circumstances.

The storytelling-preacher should select life-lessons to include in a sermon by considering:
- All life-lessons discovered in the Bible story
- Greatest needs in the lives of listeners
- Select life-lessons that best connect with the needs of listeners

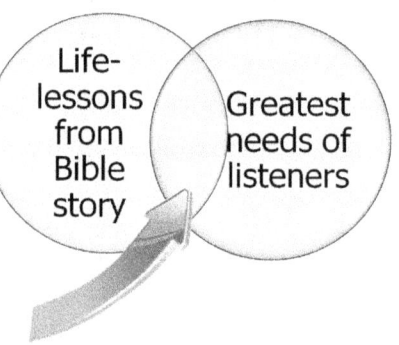

I recommend that for each sermon, the storytelling-preacher choose between two and four life-lessons to develop. Most of the time two or three life-lessons will be sufficient. The more life-lessons the preacher sends out, the less the listeners will take home.

PREACHING CYCLE

The **Preaching Cycle** is an excellent tool to elaborate on life-lessons discovered in the story and selected to be utilized as sermon points. More detailed information on the **Preaching Cycle** is found in the chapter "ADD FLAVOR WITH STORY SPICES."

After selecting the life-lessons he wishes to communicate, he will use the **Preaching Cycle** with each one. The **Preaching Cycle** requires three activities for each life-lesson selected to become a sermon division:

- 1st **Explain** life-lesson
- 2nd **Illustrate** life-lesson with another story
- 3rd **Apply** life-lesson to the lives of the listeners

1st Explain the life-lesson

During explanation, ideas reign. Explanation is analytical in nature and communicates ideas following the path of reason.

Some of the things the storytelling preacher does while explaining the life-lesson are:
- State the life-lesson and elaborate on how the story reveals the life-lesson. Events from the text-story help explain the life-lesson.
- Clarify details and present facts about the Bible story that make the life-lesson more understandable.
- Give information that helps listeners clearly understand the life-lesson.

- Use other Bible texts that help explain and reinforce the life-lesson. The Bible interprets itself. Therefore, the preacher can use other teaching texts to explain the life-lesson being emphasized.
Example: Verses from Psalms, Proverbs, Jesus' teachings, Paul's letters, the General Epistles and Hebrews can be used to explain a life-lesson discovered in a Bible story.

2nd Illustrate the life-lesson

During illustration, story reigns. Stories illustrate the idea of the sermon division.

Each sermon division may be illustrated with events from other Bible stories or from stories outside the Bible.

Types of Illustrations:
- Bible stories other than the story that is the text
- Stories outside the Bible
- Jokes
- Personal experiences
- Other people's experiences
- Works of arts–theater, films, TV, novels, paintings
- Literature, published stories
- Sports events
- Historical events
- Contemporary events

Attention:
- A good sermon illustration is usually short and simple.
- Use illustrations that link to things the listeners know and have experienced.
Example: Don't use farm illustrations with people who have always lived in the city.
- A storyteller is successful when entertaining, but a storytelling-preacher is effective only when stories help communicate biblical truths.

3rd **Apply the life-lesson to the listeners' lives**

An application establishes what God desires the listeners to know, to be, or to do as a result of understanding the life-lesson discovered in the Bible story.

Application explains how the listeners should change by putting the life-lessons presented into personal action.

3. Conclusion to the Sermon

Preach so that people will believe something—conclude so that when they believe, they will do something.
- Preach so people will believe
- Conclude so people will act

The wise preacher knows to conclude his sermon before listeners wish he would shut-up! He needs to know how long listeners will listen to him. Once when I was in the rural interior of Brazil, a lady angrily told me, "I didn't walk two and a half hours to church just to hear a thirty minute sermon." Once in Brazil and again in Mexico, I was strongly criticized because I only preached for forty-five minutes. In India, I was told that I was expected to speak for two hours and fifteen minutes. Different cultures and communities have different expectations for sermon length. The preacher should stop preaching before his listeners stop listening. Many congregations have internal stopwatches. Some listeners will stop listening at noon no matter what the preacher is saying. Other congregations give the preacher twenty, twenty-five, thirty-five or forty-five minutes; then they will tune him out. The preacher should conclude before listeners tune him out. Land the plane before listeners open the hatch with a mental parachute to bail out.

The preacher should end his sermon in such a way that it lives on. The preacher ends his sermon with the conclusion; however, listeners begin another week of facing daily life-issues; wrestling with spiritual adversaries in heavenly places; wrestling with daily life issues at home, school or work; fighting their own human nature that wants them to make wrong choices.

The preacher needs to learn from the fisherman. If fish don't bite on one bait, the fisherman tries another. Sometimes he uses live bait – a worm, or a cricket; sometimes he uses artificial bait – a spinner or a fly. His bait depends on where he's fishing and what he's trying to catch. The fisherman doesn't bait his hook with what he happens to like best or is most used to using; rather, he uses whatever lands the most fish. Preachers must be as wise in preparing sermon conclusions, varying techniques and trying new approaches when "fishing" for men and women for Christ.

The preacher who preaches a sermon without knowing how to end it is like a pilot taking off in a plane without knowing how to land it. The preacher stops his sermon with the conclusion, and he needs to learn the art of ending his sermon.

The conclusion is where the preacher closes the deal and presses for decisions of commitment based on his text and sermon points preached. The lawyer is considered to have failed if he eloquently argues his case; however, his closing arguments fail to draw forth a positive verdict even though his client deserves restitution. The car salesman who makes a fluent sales presentation but doesn't close and make a sale will go hungry and won't make house payments. Preachers must learn the art of concluding. It's important that the sermon beginning grasps listeners' attention. It's important that the oral Bible story inspires listeners to compare themselves to the key-characters and their situations. It's important that sermon life-lessons both instruct and inspire. It's equally important that the sermon conclusion helps listeners decide what action they're going to take. The preacher must close for Christ; he must concentrate on the verdict.

1st The conclusion should summarize:
- The principal facts of the Bible story
- The principal life-lessons (divisions of the sermon) presented

2nd The conclusion should invite listeners to change by putting the truths and applications presented into action

The conclusion should have two basic parts that preachers should always include, and they should be in their right order. The first part of the conclusion should be a summary of the sermon. The last part ought to be a call to action.

The first part of the conclusion should be a summary of the story-text and sermon points. Restate sermon major points forcefully, but don't re-preach the sermon again. The sermon summary reviews and informs the mind. The call to action confronts the will.

The second part of the conclusion presses for a verdict. The preacher who uses the Preaching Cycle with every life-lesson develops application throughout his sermon. But, the conclusion should make stronger application, prevailing upon listeners to take action. The sermon that doesn't call for action is a message without a purpose. Good conclusions lead listeners to change their lives. The call to action challenges each listener to interact with the Bible story and act on life-lessons presented during the sermon. The call for action should be specific about what listeners should do. Unless the conclusion is specific and clear, people will be confused about what action to take. Ask for a specific response. Nothing becomes dynamic until it becomes specific. All sermon conclusions should have a common goal: to get listeners to change and do something.

The common goal of all sermon conclusions should be to get the listeners to change! The desired change may include one or more of the following areas:
- Emotional
- Intellectual
- Behavioral
- Physical

but change must occur for the sermon to be successful.

The preacher wants his listeners to change in one or more of the following ways:
- Believe a truth they haven't believed
- Understand a truth they haven't understood
- Trust a promise they haven't trusted
- Obey a command or law they haven't been obeying

- Become something they haven't been
- Do something they haven't been doing

The conclusion should be short. It should take less than ten percent of the sermon. A thirty minute sermon could have a three minute conclusion. The conclusion should be short and powerful! The conclusion should be similar to Espresso coffee served in New Orleans:
- Strong (powerful)
- Hot (animated)
- Sweet (leave a good taste)
- Little (short)

EXAMPLE: Bible story followed by sermon divisions utilizing Preaching Points

DAVID'S BETRAYAL OF GOD AND FRIENDS
BIBLE STORY USING INTERLOCKING FACTS FOUND IN CROSS-REFERENCES
David's Sin with Bathsheba (2 Samuel 11:1 - 12:14)
(Cross-References – 2 Samuel 16: 23; 23:34, 39)

BIBLE STORY
Initial-situation (*Includes the back-story*)

King Saul became the first king of Israel. However, on two occasions King Saul disobeyed the Lord, and the Lord rejected Saul as king. The Lord sent prophet Samuel to anoint young David as king. King Saul tried to kill David; David lived as a fugitive in wilderness hideouts with Saul pursuing him.

The Philistines made war on Saul's army and King Saul died in battle. The tribe of Judah immediately anointed David as their king. After seven years, all the tribes of Israel anointed David as king.

King David's men captured Jerusalem and he took up residence there. King David became more powerful because the Lord was with him. Foreign governments made treaties with King David.

King David wanted to build a temple for the Lord. The Lord told David that he wouldn't build a temple, but his son would. The

Lord promised to establish David's kingdom forever. King David reigned over all Israel, doing what was just and right for all his people.

King David had victory every time he and his army faced enemies in battle.

(*Interlocking cross-reference*)

The following event shows David's Mighty Warriors' loyalty. Once, a band of enemies surrounded David. David was thirsty and longed for water and said, "Oh, that someone would get me water from the well near the gate of Bethlehem!" Three Mighty Warriors slipped through enemy lines, drew water from the well near the gate of Bethlehem, and brought it back to David. David refused to drink the water; instead, he poured it out as a gift to the Lord. David said, "I couldn't drink this water; men risked their lives to get it!" (2 Sam 23:13-17).

Bible story: David's Sin with Bathsheba

It was the custom for kings to go off to war in the spring time. King David dispatched his commander-in-chief with the king's soldiers to war, but David stayed in Jerusalem (2 Sam 11:1).

After lunch one afternoon, King David took a nap. David got up from his nap and walked around on the flat roof of his palace. From the vantage point of the roof, David looked down and saw a beautiful woman bathing. David asked a man about the woman. The man reported, "She's Bathsheba, Eliam's daughter and Uriah's wife" (2 Sam 11:2-3).

King David didn't know Bathsheba; however, he knew her family. Eliam, Bathsheba's father, was one of David's elite Thirty Mighty Warriors (2 Sam 23:34). Ahithophel, Eliam's father and Bathsheba's grandfather, was David's chief counselor. David considered that Ahithophel's counsel was the very words of God (2 Sam 16:23). Uriah, Bathsheba's husband, was also one of David's elite Thirty Mighty Warriors (2 Sam 23:39).

King David sent messengers to fetch Bathsheba. She came to him; David and Bathsheba went to bed. Bathsheba returned home. Later, Bathsheba sent word to David, "I'm pregnant" (2 Sam 11:4-5).

David sent word for his army's commander-in-chief to send Uriah, Bathsheba's husband, to Jerusalem. Warrior Uriah arrived and David requested information about the war. Then David told Uriah, "Go to your house and have a good night's sleep."
Uriah left the palace, but slept on a mat, at the palace entrance with David's servants. Uriah didn't go home.
The next morning, David asked Uriah, "Why didn't you go home?"
Uriah answered, "My commander-in-chief and fellow soldiers are sleeping in tents. My duties as an officer during a time of war, kept me from going home to sleep with my wife!"
David told Uriah, "Stay here today; tomorrow I'll send you back." However, the next day, David invited Uriah to eat the evening meal with him. David got Uriah drunk. But, Uriah still didn't go home; Uriah slept on his mat at the palace entrance with David's servants (2 Sam 11:6-13).

The next morning, David wrote a letter to his commander-in-chief and sent it with Uriah. David wrote his commander-in-chief, "Put Uriah in the front line where the fighting is most fierce. Let him be killed in battle" (2 Sam 11:14-16).

Bathsheba heard that her husband Uriah was dead. Bathsheba grieved for her husband Uriah. After the time of mourning was over, David sent for Bathsheba and she became David's wife. Bathsheba gave birth to David's son. But, the Lord didn't like what David had done (2 Sam 11:26-27).

The Lord sent prophet Nathan to David. Prophet Nathan told David, "There were two men in the same town, one rich and the other poor. The rich man had many sheep and cattle, but the poor man had nothing except one little female lamb which he bought and raised. It grew up with the poor man's children. It shared his food, drank from his cup and even slept in his arms. The lamb was like a daughter to him. Now a traveler stopped to visit the rich man. But, the rich man was too stingy to take one of his own sheep or cattle to feed the traveler. Instead, the rich man took the poor man's one lamb and cooked it for his guest to eat."

King David exploded with anger and told Nathan, "The rich man who did this deserves to die! The rich man must pay for that lamb four times over for his crime and his stinginess!"

Prophet Nathan told David, "You are the man! This is what the Lord, the God of Israel, says, `I made you king over Israel; I saved you from King Saul; I gave you King Saul's daughter and other wives; I gave you both Israel and Judah. Why did you ignore the Lord's command and do this great evil? You murdered Uriah with the sword of your enemy, and you took Uriah's wife as your wife! Now, the sword will never depart from your house, murder and killing will continually plague your family. I'm going to bring calamity upon you out of your own family. I'll take your wives and give them to one who is close to you, and he'll lie with your wives in broad daylight. You did it in secret, but I'll do it to you in broad daylight with all of Israel watching.'"

David told Prophet Nathan, "I've sinned against the Lord."

Nathan replied, "The Lord forgives your sin. You're not going to die for it. Your sin made the Lord's enemies lose all respect for him; therefore, the son born to you will die" (2 Sam 12:1-14).

SERMON DIVISIONS

1. Sexual sin: so easy the act, so painful the result.

Explanation:

It was so easy for David to go to bed with Bathsheba (2 Sam 11:4); however, the results were painfully long lasting (2 Sam 12:9-14). The consequences of David's sin were irreversible. To hide his sin, David planned the murder of Bathsheba's husband, an innocent man. David's son Amnon saw his father take the wife of another man, and Amnon raped his half-sister (2 Sam 13:1-23). Absalom knew that his father had an innocent man murdered, and Absalom murdered his brother who was guilty of incest/rape (2 Sam 13:28-29). Absalom saw his father usurp the place of Uriah (2 Sam 11:3), and Absalom decided to usurp his father's throne (2 Sam 15:1-13).

Giving in to impulses to misuse sex brings disastrous consequences.

People have impulses to misuse sex. Unmarried youth feel that the sex act would be the ultimate thrill. Most married people feel that the act with someone other than their spouse would be more exciting. Some people have desires for people of the same gender. Some adults have desires for children or youth. Some youth and adults feel impulses to look at pornography. The impulse to misuse sex only considers promised pleasure, not the painful consequences.

Illustration:
On one occasion, I felt that a lady was too friendly. I felt the impulse that to respond to her friendliness would bring pleasure. I prayed that God would make me aware of the way my wife would sob if I were unfaithful. I prayed that I could feel the anger my sons would feel if I betrayed them and their mother. I prayed that I could feel the deception church members would feel if I betrayed my wife, and that I would hear the sarcasm and jokes unchurched people would tell about me if I became unfaithful.

A Christian was asleep in a hammock in the Amazon forest under a big tree. He awoke feeling a weight upon his chest. He was horrified to discover that a snake, seeking warmth, had coiled up upon his chest. The man had the impulse to jump and knock the snake away; however, he knew if he moved, the snake would bite him. The man prayed, "Lord, keep me from following my impulses."

Application:
The Christian who feels impulses to misuse sex should also pray, "Lord, keep me from following my impulses." You do not choose the way you are tempted, but you do choose how you will respond to your temptations. Giving in to our impulses to misuse sex brings disastrous consequences to us and to others.

2. Wrong committed against a person is sin against God.

Explanation:
David betrayed two of his Mighty Warriors: Eliam, Bathsheba's father (2 Sam 23:34); Uriah, Bathsheba's husband (2 Sam 23:39). Also, David betrayed his chief counselor, Ahithophel, Bathsheba's grandfather (2 Sam 16:23).

Illustration:
Genesis 39 tells the story of Joseph in Potiphar's house. Joseph was Potiphar's slave. Joseph was well-built and good looking. Potiphar's wife invited Joseph to go to bed with her. Joseph asked her, "How can I do such a wicked thing and sin against God" (Gen 39:9 NIV). Joseph knew that to betray his master was to sin against God.

Application:
We need to watch and pray that we do not betray family and friends, because to wrong another person is to sin against God.

3. A spiritual leader's sin causes people to lose respect for God.

Explanation:
Prophet Nathan told David that his sin caused the Lord's enemies to show contempt for the Lord (2 Sam 12:14).

A spiritual leader's sin causes people to lose respect for God. The apostle Peter was speaking about false teachers in the church and said, "Many will follow their shameful ways and will bring the way of the truth into disrepute" (2 Peter 2:2 NIV).

Illustration:
I watched on TV the 2010 SEC championship football game with Auburn against South Carolina. Cam Newton was Auburn's quarterback. Several times TV cameras showed Cam Newton's mother cheering for her son. Each time the commentator mentioned that Cecil Newton Sr., Cam's father, could not attend the game because Auburn didn't want Cecil near its program. The reason – Cecil tried to sell his son for $180,000 to the Mississippi State Bulldogs, and when caught, he lied about his actions. The commentator always added, "And he's a preacher."

Cecil Newton Sr. became another preacher who gives people cause to use in the argument, "If the preacher lives a lie, how can we believe that the preacher preaches the truth?" Cecil added to the mistrust people feel toward preachers, the church and God.

I'm also a preacher. I fear that one day I will act on my greed, lust, anger, or road rage, and those who talk about me will add, "And, he's a preacher!"

I was in high school and we had a Sunday School teacher whom we loved. Every weekend he helped us youth type up the Sunday bulletin and duplicate them in the mimeograph machine. He constantly had us in his home and he did different fun activities with us. One weekend, a teenage girl from our Sunday School class was babysitting at a party where our Sunday School teacher was present and he became drunk. The event caused the teenage girl to question the church.

Application:
We who are spiritual leaders, parents in our home, staff members of a church, deacons, and Sunday School teachers need to watch and pray, because one consequence of our falling into sin is others will lose respect for our God.

4. Confessed sin is forgiven; however, its consequences will endure.

Explanation:
The person who sows his wild oats and, at the time of harvest, prays for a crop failure will have his prayer denied by God. The person who drives in the fast lane and prays that he won't get caught will have his prayer denied by God. David confessed his sin and was forgiven; however, he suffered the consequences of his sin (2 Sam 12:10-14).

The apostle John promised, "If we confess our sins, he is faithful and just and will forgive us our sins and purify us from all unrighteousness" (1 John 1:9 NIV).

Illustration:
I have low tolerance for milk products. Too much milk gives me an upset stomach. But, I love ice cream. There have been times when my wife would bring home a bucket of ice-cream and I, by myself, would eat half the bucket. I'd then feel guilty and ask God to forgive me for abusing my body, which is the Temple of

the Holy Spirit. God would forgive me; however, I still suffered severe stomach cramps for a couple of days.

Application:
Confessed sin is forgiven; however, undesirable consequences of sin will endure. If you have fallen into sin, confess your sins and receive God's forgiveness. But, you need to be aware that you will still suffer on this earth some consequences of your sin.

One of the reasons we need to watch and pray is that resisting impulses to sin protects us from undesirable consequences that disobeying God brings.

CONCLUSION

1. We need to watch and pray. It's easy to give into strong impulses and use sex outside of marriage. We don't break God's commands, but disobeying God's commands will break us. Misusing sex will bring painful consequences.
2. We need to watch and pray so that we do not betray or wrong other people. To wrong another person is to sin against God.
3. We who are parents in our home, staff members of a church, deacons, and Sunday School teachers are spiritual leaders. We need to watch and pray, because one consequence of our falling into sin is that others will lose respect for our God.
4. Give praise to God that he forgives us when we confess our sins. If you have fallen into sin, confess your sins and receive God's forgiveness. But, you need to be aware that you will still suffer some consequences of your forgiven sin. One of the reasons we need to watch and pray is that resisting impulses to sin protects us from the undesirable consequences that disobeying God brings.

SERVING A BIBLE STORY
Bible Storytelling Performance

Our dining room table is large enough to comfortably seat ten people. If my wife prepares a meal for ten or less people, she puts the prepared food on the table and expects everyone to pass all dishes from the left. In years past, guests and servers passed dishes from the left, because most people are right-handed. Passing from the left allowed each person to serve themselves from the dish while it was being held by the passer. Nowadays, in many homes, the passer seldom continues to hold the dish; the passer expects the person sitting next to him to take the dish, place it beside his own plate, and serve himself.

If my wife serves a large crowd at our house, she puts different dishes of food on a serving table and/or counter spaces. Then she gives guests the responsibility of serving their own plates.

The expository storytelling-preacher serves the Bible story to his listeners by giving a public performance of the story. He performs the story to give an authentic presentation of Scripture, not to put on a show.

God's Message Can Be Just the Bible Story

The Bible makes this claim about God's Word, "My word that goes out from my mouth, it will not return to me empty, but will accomplish what I desire" (Isaiah 55:11 NIV). The promise is that God's Word will not return empty; however, the preacher is not promised that his interpretation of God's Word will not return empty. Bible stories are God's stories. A simple Bible story that is well-told is a powerful story and will not return empty. Often it is appropriate to just tell a Bible story, without any interpretation after the story. Trust that God will accomplish what he desires with his story.

There are many long Bible stories that I have condensed into less than a thirty minute story. When it is time for me to preach, I just tell the Bible story. I don't explain the story. I don't mention the moral of the story. I don't mention life-lessons found in the story. I tell the story without any interpretation. I just tell the story. When I finish the story, I'm finished with my presentation.

Examples of long stories that can be told as God's Message:
- Christmas story. Often on the Sunday before Christmas, I harmonize the events recorded in Matthew chapters 1-2 and Luke chapters 1-2 into one story. The telling of Jesus' birth takes about 27 minutes. When I finish the story of the first Christmas, I'm finished. I stop without making any interpretation.
- The appearances of Jesus after his resurrection. On the Sunday after Easter, I like to harmonize into one story the ten appearances of Jesus after his resurrection. The story takes about 30 minutes to tell. When I finish the story, I'm finished. The emotional impact of this story is powerful.
- Abraham's story
- Joseph's story
- David's story
- First year of Jesus' public ministry
- Events of Passover week that terminate with Jesus' crucifixion
- Paul's missionary journeys

God's Message Can Be a Bible Story Followed by Interpretation

The expository Bible storytelling-preacher can tell a short Bible story followed by outlining a list of life-lessons discovered in the Bible story. The preacher starts his sermon by performing a short Bible story. Many Bible stories can be told in two to five minutes. Others may take ten to fifteen minutes.

After performing the Bible story, the expository Bible storytelling-preacher extracts life-lessons from the story and develops them into sermon points.

Plan for Expository Bible Story Sermon

1st Bible Story Performed Orally

The preacher does not need to prepare an introduction for an expository Bible story sermon. He begins by performing the Bible story. The only introduction needed is something similar to:

- "I'm going to tell you a story found in the Bible, Exodus, chapters 1-4."
- "I'm going to tell you an old, old story, but it is a true story that is found in the Bible."
- "I'm going to tell you a true story from the Bible that can change your life."

Then the storytelling-preacher performs the Bible story accurately and completely.

2nd Sermon Divisions Utilizing Preaching Points

After narrating the Bible story accurately and completely, the expository storytelling-preacher develops life-lessons discovered in the story into sermon points. Every spoken word from the pulpit amplifies, elaborates, or illustrates life-lessons discovered in the story.

Chapter 5, **Adding Flavor with Story Spices** gives suggestions on how to develop each sermon point.

3rd Conclusion

Preparing to Perform a Bible Story

The Bible storyteller must prepare to perform. The storyteller must commit to prepare. The storyteller who fails to prepare, prepares to fail. Don't think you can tell a familiar story without preparation. Bible storytelling requires preparation and work to accurately tell the story and have it come alive for listeners. The storyteller who stands like a statue and recites the verbal content of a story with the same speaking voice is dull and flat. He must go beyond telling the story; he must perform the story.

If the storyteller plans to retell a story he knows, he still needs to prepare for the new telling. When my wife prepares a meal for guests, she always has leftovers that she puts into the refrigerator. The next day she reheats the leftovers before serving them. In the same way, a storyteller needs to reheat a previously told story before telling it again.

Prepare to Avoid Common Mistakes of Literates

Everybody has storytelling experience. Until children started kindergarten, they mainly communicated by storytelling. However, literacy tends to choke storytelling. Often, the more literate a person becomes, the more dysfunctional he becomes as a storyteller. Education tends to diminish a person's skills of storytelling.

1. Don't assume your listeners know the story

I recently heard a preacher preach from 1 Kings 18 about Elijah on Mount Carmel. The preacher read a couple of verses from the story and began his outline with truths discovered from the story. But, he didn't tell us the story. He assumed we knew the story. Listeners who were unfamiliar with the story of Elijah on Mount Carmel would not have understood what the preacher was talking about.

Many listeners who grew up as children going to church every Sunday don't know the Bible stories. It's certain that listeners who did not grow up going to church regularly do not know most Bible stories. The preacher who refers to a Bible story should assume that many listeners are biblically illiterate and unfamiliar with Bible stories. He should take time to tell the story.

2. Don't rush to the core of the story

Many preachers don't take time to accurately tell a complete Bible story. They quickly summarize the story, leaving out most details and sequence of events found in the story. They rush to the core of the story in order to get to the main life-lesson of the story.

Storytellers and story-listeners get inside the story and experience it. They picture characters, scenes, events, emotions, and actions. Literate thinkers often observe the story from the outside, evaluate it and look for the point of the story instead of taking a story-journey, experiencing the story. Do not quickly summarize the story; do perform the story!

3. Don't insert interpretation into the story

One of the most difficult things for beginning literate storytelling-preachers is to overcome the habit of interjecting explanations during the narrating of the story. The highly literate storyteller tends to explain the story instead of telling it. He tends to constantly interrupt the telling of the story to interpret it. An entertaining storyteller does not interrupt his story to give explanation, nor does he interrupt the story to ask questions to verify his listeners are getting the main point of the story. During the process of narrating a Bible story, don't tell listeners your interpretation of the story; don't add personal commentary; don't add a moral truth as a part of the story. Just tell the story.

4. Don't recreate the story

Be accurate. The expository Bible storyteller should be true to the facts in the Bible text. Be exact in order not to mislead.

- Don't embellish the story. Don't exaggerate and recreate the story – inventing facts, situations and events not found in the biblical narrative.
  Example of what not to do:
  Do not embellish the story of the flood (Genesis 6 - 8). Do not narrate that Noah's neighbors climbed on floating tree trunks, paddled to the ark, beat on the door screaming, "Noah, open the door, it's us, your neighbors!"
- Don't try to bring a Bible story up to date and place it into a modern setting.
  Example of what not to do:
  Do not modernize the story of Joseph's temptation with Potiphar's wife (Genesis 39). Joseph becomes a university student. Potiphar becomes Joseph's middle aged, primary professor. Potiphar's wife becomes the young trophy and eye-candy wife of Professor Potiphar. Potiphar's wife wants Joseph to satisfy her sexual appetites in ways that her middle aged husband can't.
- Be cautious with children's Bible story books, films, or dramas that take liberty with Bible stories. One lady in a Bible storytelling group had a CD library for her children that contained all the VeggieTales movies. Whenever she told a Bible story, she followed the story-line from a VeggieTale movie instead of accurately following the Bible.

5. Don't defend God's Word

The storytelling-preacher does not need to defend God's Words and actions when he tells Bible stories. He should narrate the story and trust God's Word to be its own defense. Paul referred to the word of God as being the "sword of the Spirit" (Ephesians 6:17). The Roman soldier in conflict would not defend his sword by naming the craftsman who made it and describing the quality of its iron. No, the Roman soldier used the sword against his enemy. There is no need to defend God's story. Tell Bible stories and trust God's Spirit to communicate God's Word.

There is a time and place for apologetics. But, the time and place is not when telling and performing a Bible story.

6. Don't read the story; tell it

Some preachers write out a manuscript of their sermon; when preaching, they read the manuscript. Stories should be told and not read. Few professional actors can read a story as well as they tell it. Stories are meant to be told. A teller can be more dynamic, has more freedom to use gestures, and can better express emotions than a reader. A teller can put himself into the story and use everything he has – his face, body, voice, sounds and words. He doesn't just tell a story; he takes the listeners along on a story-journey.

7. Don't use a public speaking voice to tell the story

I recently heard a preacher speak for twenty minutes and do an excellent job of interpreting his text. He used an authoritative, loud public speaking voice the entire time. When he narrated a story, he maintained the same public speaking voice without changing his rate or pitch of speech. Some preachers use a public speaking voice whenever they preach. Instead of telling a story, they preach the story. Storytelling requires a conversational voice, similar to the way a person talks when he is sitting around a dinner table telling a story to friends.

Suggestions on How to Prepare to Perform a Story

1. Understand that storytelling has three essential components

- **A story** – Bible stories were told orally before they were written. The written story was recorded to be understood and remembered when read aloud. Stories are meant to be told.
- **A teller** – The teller puts himself into the story. He feels empathy for the story and uses everything he has – his

face, body, voice, sounds and words; because, he doesn't just tell a story, he shares it with his listeners.
- **Listeners** – Storytelling requires a face-to-face interaction between the storyteller and the story-listeners.

2. The storytelling-preacher needs to prepare in advance

The storytelling-preacher who fails to prepare, prepares to fail. The storyteller's preparation contributes to the success of a story. Discipline and preparation do not destroy the spontaneity of storytelling. Discipline and practice are as important to the storyteller as they are to other artists such as musicians, tap-dancers, singers, actors, and clowns. The storyteller must exercise discipline and practice in order to perform with ease.

The following suggestions will help the storyteller prepare in advance for telling his story.
- Begin preparation by analyzing the story several days before telling it.
- Read and reread the story in the Bible each day for several days in advance of the telling. I suggest reading the story in different translations. Also, daily review one's analysis of the story.

3. Learn the story; avoid memorizing the story

The act of memorizing the story instills the fear of forgetting it. The memorized story makes the listeners uneasy. My memory has failed me in the past, and I would be stupid to expect it not to ever fail me in the future. If a teller has memorized a story and he forgets a word or phrase, he is lost and may need to start over again.

4. It is helpful to memorize a few key parts of the story

- Memorize the beginning. The storyteller who has memorized his first sentences is able to begin strong.
- Memorize the ending. The storyteller who has memorized his last sentences knows when he is finished, and he is able to end strong.

- Memorize phrases that are repeated.
  Example: In the creation story several phrases are repeated and need to be memorized:
  - God said..., and it was so (1:3, 6, 9, 11, 14, 20, 24).
  - There was evening, and there was morning (1:3, 6, 11, 19, 23, 31).
  - God saw that it was good (1:4, 10, 12, 18, 21, 25, 31).
- Memorize lists that are contained within the story. Most stories do not contain lists, but some do. If a story contains a list, the storyteller either needs a cheat sheet or he must memorize the list. Story mapping with stick figures that represent each item in the list can be a helpful tool. It is best to quote the list from memory.
  Examples:
  - The creation story has seven days and the creation events of each day need to be memorized (Genesis 1-2).
  - God sent ten plagues against the Egyptians when he was forcing Egypt to let the descendants of Israel leave enslavement in Egypt (Exodus 7:8 - 12:34).
  - The ten commandments need to be memorized in order (Exodus 20:1-17).

5. Think and rethink the story before telling it

The storyteller uses his imagination in order to understand what happened and feel the emotions of the story; however, he doesn't use his imagination to reinvent what happened! He needs to use his imagination to experience the story he will be telling: the sights; the sounds; the smells; the tastes; the feelings; the emotions. Before telling a story, I use my imagination and try to experience the story. I try to dream the story and see the story as though it were a film playing on the screen of my mind.

6. Map out the Bible story using visual symbols

Mapping out the Bible story using stick line drawings helps the storyteller visualize and remember it. Instead of writing words and sentences, represent each event of the story with a design or a stick line drawing. This helps the storyteller see the story in picture blocks, not in words. Thinking in pictures helps the storyteller see the story better than remembering words. The story map is for the storyteller and not for the listeners.

When it is time to perform the story, if the teller needs a cheat-sheet, it is better to glance at a stick drawing on the story map than to read words.

7. **Pantomime the Bible story**

Pantomiming is an excellent tool for learning a Bible story without memorizing it.

When our family first moved to Brazil, I didn't speak the language and used pantomiming to communicate to salespeople and they pantomimed to me. To buy eggs, I put my fingers from my two hands together to form an oval shape. Then I put my hands by my side and flapped them as if they were wings, and I clucked like a chicken.

The pantomime communicates through body movement instead of the spoken word. It communicates a thought, action, object, or event by means of body movements, gestures, facial expressions and attitudes. *Example*: One would pantomime the idea of a baby by cradling an imaginary infant.

To pantomime a story, the storyteller uses the full range of movement allowed by the human body to express each thought, attitude, dialogue, object, and event found in the story. He mimes the story without uttering spoken words.

As the storyteller prepares to tell his story, I suggest that the storyteller pantomime the Bible story in two stages:
- 1st First stage: While reading the Bible story, use gestures and facial expressions to express each sequence of events in the story.
- 2nd Second stage: Close the Bible and remember each story detail without memorizing it. At this point, minimize the spoken word by saying few words while concentrating

on pantomiming each event and dialogue with gestures and body movement.

Pantomiming the story builds memory muscles for the storyteller.

8. Story performance involves the whole body

The storyteller merges his whole being into the story he is telling. Storytelling performance combines:

- **Verbal expressions** – (Using words to craft the story for telling) The crafted story must be true to the Bible story. The storyteller needs to tell the story and only the story.

- **Gestures** – (Using visual non-verbal communication) Gestures may include eye expressions, facial expressions, movement of hands and feet, and expressive movement. Gestures allow the storyteller to communicate a variety of feelings and thoughts, from contempt and hostility to approval and affection. *Example:* Hand gestures can clearly communicate the following: come, go, good-bye, yes, no, and so forth without a spoken word.

- **Posture** – (Posing or bearing of the body for the purpose of expressing attitudes) A teller may assume a different posture to express different characters.

- **Movement** – (Moving around from one stage position to another) Movement can help the storyteller portray characters, moods, attitudes, and events. Movement should be done intentionally and purposefully. Movement involves walking from one stage location to another stage location. It also involves changing body position, such as standing, sitting, kneeling, facing forward or turning to the side.

    A useful movement tool is the **Storytelling V** – The storyteller faces his listeners directly when he narrates the story. However, when he narrates a dialogue, he uses the **Storytelling V** to show how the conversation passes from one character to another. The storyteller faces one direction, as though he were looking at one Bible character, and speaks to him. Then he pivots slightly to the side to face his previous character to speak for the second Bible character. He switches positions each time a different character speaks. Also, use the **Storytelling V** to show social standing. When quoting the more important character speaking to an inferior, look slightly down; when an inferior is speaking to his superior, look slightly up.

Example: If I were telling the story of King David's sin (2 Samuel 11), when I quote King David speaking to soldier Uriah, I look slightly to the right and down; when I quote soldier Uriah speaking to King David, I look slightly to the left and up.

- **Eye contact** – (Looking into the eyes of one's listeners) The eyes are as important for non-verbal communication as the mouth is for verbal communication. I often see preachers looking at their PowerPoint slides, their notes, or their manuscripts; they rarely look at their listeners. The storyteller needs to look his listeners in the eyes. He should look at their facial expressions and their reactions to his story. If the preacher wants to know if people are listening, he should look into their eyes. Looking listeners in the eye helps the storyteller talk to people as if he were in a one-on-one conversation. It helps the storyteller come across as conversational. That makes him easy to listen to and engaging.

If you want to know if someone is listening to you, look into their eyes. As listeners listen with the eyes, they respond by sending signals. And the preacher should speak to what he sees in listeners' eyes.

I often see the sticker on a big truck, "If you can't see my mirror, I can't see you." If the storyteller can't see the eyes of his listeners, they can't see his eyes nor his mouth. The storytelling-preacher may need to move around on stage to find a location where he can best see his listeners' eyes and where he can best be seen.

The storytelling-preacher who doesn't use eye contact might as well FedEx his message to his listeners.

However, the exception is when the storyteller is using the **Storytelling V** to show how dialogue passes from one character to another. The storyteller faces one direction as though he were looking at one Bible character and speaks to him. Then he pivots slightly to the side to face his previous character to speak for the second Bible character. He switches positions each time a different character speaks.

- **Eye movements** – (Moving the eyes to look in different locations) Eye movement can suggest the relationship between a character and the objects or people with whom the character interacts. Eye movements can suggest the relationship between a superior character to an inferior character. The inferior character looks up to the superior and the superior looks down to the inferior. Eye movement can suggest spatial perspective–the location where a person is standing or where an object is located. Eye movement can suggest attitude signals: looking upward can signal doubt or unbelief; looking downward can express embarrassment, modesty, or shame.

    The **Storytelling V** requires eye movement to show how the conversation passes from one character to another.

- **Spatial perspective** – (Determining where scenes, persons or objects are located on the storytelling stage) The storyteller should plan the spatial perspective for the stage where he performs. He should determine a location on the stage for each scene, person, object, or location mentioned in the story.

- *Example:* If I'm telling the creation story (Genesis 1 - 2), I'll come to the third day when God gathered the waters into seas and dry land appeared. In my mind, I'll designate a location on stage for the seas and another for dry land. When I tell the fifth day of creation, I'll point toward the stage location for the seas when I speak of God making water creatures and I'll point toward the stage location for dry land when I speak of God making birds. When I tell the sixth day of creation and God creating the animals and people, I'll point toward the stage location for dry land.
- *Example*: If I'm telling the story of Jesus' birth, I'll select a location on stage for Nazareth, another for Bethlehem, another for Jerusalem, and another for Egypt.

- **Facial expressions** – (Using muscles in the face to convey emotions and feelings) A storyteller can use just the face to express non-verbal communication. A smile can signal approval or happiness; a frown can signal disapproval or unhappiness. The face must express the emotions that correspond to the spoken words of the story. If telling a sad story, the storyteller's face should look sad. *Example:* when telling the story of Jesus' crucifixion, tears are more appropriate than a grin.

- **Voice** – (Using modulation of the storyteller's voice: low pitch – high pitch, fast, slow, loud, soft, whisper, old person, young person, etc.) Storytelling is basically normal conversation elevated for effective communication. Voice includes:
  - **Tone** – (Alteration in pitch of the voice) Tone may be modulated to suggest emotions such as anger, surprise, or happiness.
  - **Volume** – (Loud to normal to soft) Volume variety gives the voice variety and expressiveness. Proper volume is necessary for listeners to hear the storyteller. He wants to make sure listeners can hear him. In many situations this requires knowing how to use a microphone.

- **Pauses** – (Silence between spoken words) Silence between words communicates volumes. Pauses can communicate more than the spoken word. Pauses can be the exclamation marks of oral speech. When quoting dialogue, pause between speakers. This helps listeners identify when one speaker stopped and another is ready to speak. Pauses between a series of connected events help listeners know when something new is about to happen. *For example*: When telling the creation story of Genesis 1 - 2, make a long pause between the telling of each day of the week.
- **Pitch** – (Highness or lowness of the voice) The storyteller can use different voices and pitches for different characters when narrating dialogue.
- **Temporal** – (Timing, vocal behavior, conversational rhythms, rhythms of dialogue, slow or fast, speech rate, sound patterns) When the storyteller desires to emphasize a word, it's better to s-t-r-e-t-c-h the word out than to increase volume.
- **Velocity** – (Variation of speech speed) Sometimes the storyteller needs to slow down; other times he needs to speed up. Dialogue should be spoken at a speed that is appropriate for the character speaking.

9. Rehearse the story

Discipline in practicing a story is as important to the storyteller as practice is important to the singer, the pianist, the dancer, the actor, the clown, or any other artist. Rehearsing out loud helps the storyteller-preacher know which parts come easily and which parts need more work. Practicing out loud fixes the story in his mind and gives him opportunity to work on his voice and gestures. Practicing out loud helps him feel at ease when time comes to perform the story. Practicing the story out loud does not hinder the storyteller's spontaneity; the opposite is true, rehearsing the story out loud helps the teller perform with the appearance of the lack of apparent effort. Rehearsing helps the storytelling-preacher tell the story in a relaxed manner.

Performing the Story

Storytelling is an art. My wife once took classes in oil painting. Doris went with her art teacher and fellow students to a beach and each painted the beach scenery. Each art student followed principles that the art teacher had given them; however, each painting was different. In a similar manner, storytelling is an art. Each Bible storyteller needs to be faithful to the Bible when performing the story; however, particular words, sentence structure, emphasis, gestures, tone, body movement and pitch will vary from storyteller to storyteller.

1. **Start narrating the initial-situation; then tell the Bible story following the sequence of events in chronological order**

The storyteller introduces the story by describing its initial-situation. He gives background information listeners need to know about the events leading up to the story, the key-characters, and the location of the story. This information is usually found in the context preceding the text that contains the Bible story.

In some stories, the initial-situation needs to include the back-story that gives the story behind the story. The back-story gives a narrative history of background information of events that were chronologically earlier than the main story.

Describe the initial-situation, ending with the initial-problem. The initial-problem is similar to a wiggling worm on a hook. The wiggling worm catches the attention of the fish and the initial-problem catches the attention of the listener. Then follow the structural order of the story, utilizing the sequence of events in chronological order. Finish with the final-situation.

The storyteller who understands the structure of the story and uses his imagination to experience the story is prepared to tell the story in a manner where his listeners will also experience it.

2. Expect to make mistakes

Professional, seasoned storytellers sometimes make mistakes. Mistakes do not distract from storytelling; however, the storyteller's negative reaction to a mistake may distract. If listeners sense the storyteller's embarrassment, they will share it. But, mistakes need not destroy the story. The storyteller can recover and mention a crucial missing detail later than planned in the story while non-essential events can be omitted altogether.

The best plan to improve one's ability to tell Bible stories is: practice, practice, and practice. The mind will become sharper at remembering details. The person who constantly tells Bible stories will never become perfect; however, he will constantly improve.

3. Trust the Bible story

One can never predict the results of a well-told Bible story, but the storyteller should expect the results to surprise him with joy. A well-told Bible story is similar to the seeds Jesus mentioned in his parable. The farmer planted the seed and it grew both during the day and night. The farmer neither understood how it grew nor saw it growing. A simple Bible story that is accurately told is a powerful story. The teller won't understand how it grows, and it is possible that he himself will not see the progress of its growing.

STORY-APPETIZER
Start with a Story to Initiate the Audience's Urge to Listen

Appetizers are small snack-size foods that are served immediately preceding a meal with the purpose of initiating the urge to eat. An appetizer can vary in size, type and taste, depending on the meal to follow. Samples of appetizers can be tasty dips, crackers and spreads, finger foods, nuts, cheese, bread with olive oil dip, small raw vegetables, or slices of fruits. An appetizer can be as simple as crackers and cheese or as formal as crab quiche before a seafood dinner.

The preacher can begin any type of sermon with a story-appetizer for the purpose of initiating the urge of his audience to listen.

I once heard a preacher say, "It's my responsibility to preach the Bible. It's the audience's responsibility to listen." I disagree. The preacher should not stand to preach with the attitude, "It's time for me to preach the Scripture. What I have to say is so important, you should pay attention!"

No, no, no! The preacher should have the attitude, "It's time for me to preach the Scripture. What I have to say is so important, I must catch your attention."

The preacher needs to catch his listeners' attention with his first sentence. A story at the beginning can catch listeners' attention.

The preacher is similar to the camper who prepared his campfire to cook a meal. He put loose dry grass on the bottom. He put dry twigs over the dry grass. He stacked dry wood over the dry twigs. Then he discovered he only had one dry match. If the one match didn't catch fire, he'd have no campfire, and he couldn't cook and serve the meal.

The sermon's first sentence is similar to the camper's one dry match. If the preacher doesn't catch his listener's attention with his first sentence, he'll build no fire under his listeners. Each listener will drift away to his own dream world. A story helps fire up listener's attention the way lighter fluid helps fire up charcoal. A story attracts listener's attention like a magnet attracts iron. Start with a story.

A pastor attended a weekend contemporary Christian festival with his youth. Twelve thousand young people from many states converged at a grassy hillside amphitheater. A famous gospel band finished its performance and a booming voice proclaimed. "And now one of America's leading youth speakers."
The young preacher stepped to the microphone, removed from his pocket a New Testament and said, "Let me read a few verses from the Bible."
The crowd stood for the reading of God's Word, but a tidal wave of thousands of young people surged for the grassy hillside behind the event. More than three thousand potential listeners responded to the young preacher's first words by fleeing the sound of his voice. They escaped to behind the crowd; some sat on blankets listening to CDs and snacking; others threw footballs or frisbees. The young preacher concluded with an invitation, and hundreds went forward to speak with counselors in a building behind the stage. The young preacher experienced both failure and success. He experienced failure when he spoke his first words and thousands of potential listeners walked out. He experienced success when he concluded and hundreds responded with Christian commitments. The young preacher experienced both a preacher's nightmare and a preacher's dream come true. He experienced a preacher's nightmare when, at his first spoken words, a fourth of his listeners walked out on him; he experienced a preacher's dream come true when, at his conclusion, hundreds made Christian commitments. But the young preacher failed to communicate to three thousand potential listeners who walked away when he spoke his first words.

The preacher should imagine that when he begins his sermon, his listeners are bored and are in a dream world of their own. Children daydream of playing video games. Men daydream of the afternoon ball game on TV, or they daydream of Monday's work, hunting, or fishing. Youth daydream about dating or checking text messages. Ladies daydream about preparing lunch, housework, scheduling next week's activities, or their work outside the home.

The last time I stood up to speak, a youth was sitting on the front row texting on his iPhone. He continued texting when I began to speak; however, when he realized I was telling a story he slipped his iPhone into his shirt pocket.

Prepare the first sentence of your sermon with the attitude that your listeners are bored, and that most wish they were somewhere else. Their thoughts aren't about the Bible. You must get their attention with your first sentence or they will get up and leave mentally. Most church congregations are more polite than the youth at the Christian music festival who physically left the audience. Most stay seated where you can see them, but their minds get up and go somewhere else.

Get listeners' attention with a fire-catching opening statement or a story-appetizer. You do not have a well-prepared sermon unless you prepare to kindle a quick flame of spontaneous interest with your first sentence. This chapter suggests you use a story-appetizer as a fire-catching opening. However, the preacher may open with a fire-catching opening statement. The preacher should always follow the principle of preparing an opening sentence that will kindle a quick flame of spontaneous interest.

If the preacher chooses to begin with a fire-catching opening sentence, he should imagine that after hearing his first sentence, listeners are saying, "Your opening sentence got my attention, but what does that have to do with me?" The preacher should follow his fire-catching opening sentence with a bridge-paragraph that connects the opening fire-catching sentence to the Scripture text and to the listeners.

- *Example of fire-catching opening sentence*: Look up. Look up! LOOK UP! *Bridge Paragraph*: Psalm 121 challenges us to have the upward look, "I lift up my eyes to the mountains—where does my help come from? My help comes from the Lord, the Maker of heaven and earth" (Psalm 121:1 NIV). Psalm 121 portrays the upward look we

Christians should have. The upward look we should have is not to the mountains, but to God who made the mountains. *(The preacher will follow the bridge-paragraph with the sermon that expounds on the text.)*

- *Example of fire-catching opening sentence*: Why do good things happen to bad people? Why do bad things happen to good people? *Bridge Paragraph*: The author of Psalm 73 asked both those questions and found the answer to his question. The psalmist tells why he asked his questions and where he found his answers: Why do good things happen to bad people? Why do bad things happen to good people? If you are asking those questions, the psalmist's answers can become your answers.*(The preacher will follow the bridge-paragraph with the sermon that expounds on the text.)*

A story-appetizer is an excellent way to have a fire-catching opener. Everybody loves a story. Start with a story; it will serve as a story-appetizer and initiate the desire for your audience to listen. A story-appetizer prepares listeners to listen more thoughtfully to what follows. The story-appetizer is similar to a wiggling worm on a hook. The wiggling worm catches the fish's attention and the story-appetizer catches listeners' attention.

A preacher should not use a story that has nothing to do with his sermon as an ice-breaker to warm up the congregation. If I'm invited as a storyteller to entertain, I'm successful if my listeners laugh and enjoy my stories. However, if I'm invited to preach and I start a sermon with a story, I'm only successful if my opening story builds a bridge to Scripture teaching.

The story-appetizer needs to relate to the Scripture-text or to one of the main ideas in your sermon. Determine the theme or point from Scripture you want your listeners to hear. Then come up with a story that illustrates your theme or Scripture point. Look for a story that becomes the vehicle to transport the spiritual truth you want listeners to hear. Find a story that deals with people facing common problems, but its overtone reaches into a biblical life-lesson you will deal with in your sermon. Choose a story that hints at the teaching found in your Scripture text or better, a story that incarnates your Sermon theme.

After you tell the opening story, imagine your listeners responding, "That was a good story, but what does it have to do with me? Why did you tell that intriguing story?" You need a bridge paragraph to answer those questions. After telling the story, construct a bridge-paragraph that builds a bridge between the story and the body of your sermon. Using a few sentences, build a bridge from the point of the story to tell your listeners how your story relates to your chosen Scripture text or sermon topic.

The story-appetizer needs two parts:
1st A story to initiate the urge of audiences to listen.
2nd A bridge-paragraph that builds a bridge between the story and the sermon.

Examples of Story Appetizers

Example #1:
The preacher is preparing to emphasize: Greed is a form of idolatry. His text is "Put to death, therefore, whatever belongs to your earthly nature: sexual immorality, impurity, lust, evil desires and greed, which is idolatry" (Colossians 3:5 NIV).

Story Appetizer: **GREED – MORE EGGS**
(The story: "Greed–More Eggs" is found in my book **Parable–Seeds; First Sowing**.*)*

Mrs. Farmer wanted more spending money. Mr. Farmer suggested, "You've got a dozen hens that are laying eggs. Each lays an egg a day. You aren't using most of the eggs. Sell the eggs and keep the money for your spending money."

Mrs. Farmer started gathering the eggs each morning and selling them to the town-folks. The town-folks liked her farm-fresh eggs better than the store-bought eggs. Mrs. Farmer noticed that each hen was laying an egg a day. She appreciated the extra spending money. Then she got to thinking, "If my hens laid more eggs, I'd have more spending money. I know what I'll do. I'll feed the hens twice as much chicken feed. Then I'll collect twice as many eggs from the hens. I'll collect from each hen, an egg each morning and another egg each night."

Mrs. Farmer put her plan into action. She started feeding the hens a double portion of chicken feed. The hens became fat and lazy, and stopped laying eggs.

Mrs. Farmer sold the fat hens to the town-folks. The following weeks, several families enjoyed fried chicken or barbeque chicken. By the time Mrs. Farmer paid the chicken feed bill, she had lost money on her hens.

Bridge-paragraph:
The greedy farm woman didn't get what she wanted, and she lost money. The greedy Christian will lose a close relationship with God. Our text describes greed as a form of idolatry. The thing desired becomes more important to a person than God.
(The preacher will follow the bridge-paragraph with the sermon that expounds on the text.)

Example # 2:
The preacher is preparing a sermon from a a portion of the Sermon on the Mount, Matthew 7:24-27, The parable of The Wise and Foolish Builders.

Story Appetizer: **WIFE TALKS TO HERSELF**
(The story: "Wife Talks to Herself," was crafted and copyrighted by me.)

I must confess, I've become worried about my wife. I've noticed that my wife is talking to herself more and more. When we are riding in the car together, my wife talks to herself; when we are sitting at the table eating, she talks to herself; when we are getting ready for bed at the same time, she talks to herself. My wife is also imagining things. At the same time that my wife is talking to herself, she imagines that I'm listening.

Bridge-paragraph:
When the wife talks and the husband doesn't listen, it will be disastrous for their marriage. When Jesus speaks and we don't listen, it will be disastrous for our lives. Jesus concluded the Sermon on the Mount with a story about the wise builder who built his house on the rock and the foolish builder who built his

house on the sand. The parable illustrates that when Jesus speaks and we don't listen, the result will be disastrous for our lives.

(The preacher will tell the parable of the Wise and Foolish Builders (Matthew 7:24-27). Then he will preach his sermon on the parable.)

It is important to capture your listeners' attention with the first sentence of your sermon. A story-appetizer will initiate the urge of your audience to listen.

It is not enough to catch your listeners' attention at the beginning of the sermon, you must keep their attention. The next chapter will explain about using stories as spices to keep your sermon appetizing.

ADDING FLAVOR WITH STORY SPICES
Spice Non-Story Texts with Story-Illustrations

Cooking with herbs and spices goes a long way to achieving a cook's desire to serve delicious food. Different herbs and spices are now readily available. It is hard to imagine what cooking would be like without the unique flavors provided by herbs, spices, and many seasonings.

The term "spice" is often used broadly to include all types of seasonings. Spices come from the barks, roots, leaves, stems, buds, seeds, or fruit of aromatic plants and trees which usually grow only in tropical countries. Pepper, allspice, cloves, nutmeg, mace, cinnamon, ginger, saffron, and turmeric are examples of spices.

For centuries, herbs and spices have been an integral part of many of the world's great cuisines. Today we take for granted black pepper and other spices over which wars were once fought. Once upon a time, only kings and very wealthy people could afford such a delicacy as cinnamon. Today all supermarkets and most small grocery stores have spice shelves offering a wonderful selection of herbs and spices.

The family cook can prepare nutritious meals without using any spices, including salt. However, the food wouldn't taste good and most family members wouldn't eat much. Therefore, nutritious meals without spices would not benefit family members who wouldn't eat them. Nutritious meals with spices will result in family members eating more.

Many listeners are post-literate, oral-visual communicators, who do not read for pleasure and primarily obtain information by electronic media. Without a dimension of storytelling that illustrates biblical teaching, the expository preacher's reflections remain so spiritual they do post-literate listeners little earthly good. They are abstract, spectral, creating little fire and not much light. The sermon without stories attracts oral-visual communicators the way a magnet attracts wood.

The preacher who constantly uses the **Preaching Cycle** will include spices in his sermon every time he illustrates biblical teaching with a story. Between 70% and 75% of the Bible is in story form. Paul's Epistles, Hebrews, and the General Epistles are not in story form. They make up about 10% of the Bible and are in academic abstract language.

Stories used as illustrations serve as spices that give seasoning to expository preaching on non-story text. A story can be the most enjoyable and effective means to share a truth. I suggest that preachers follow this principle: Only preach a biblical truth when you have a story to illustrate it. If a preacher really understands a biblical teaching, no matter how complex it may be, he should be able to illustrate it with a story.

An analysis of the communication styles of Jesus and Paul shows that Jesus was a storytelling preacher while Paul was an educated literate abstract communicator.

Jesus always told parables, which were short fiction-stories, to the crowds when he taught (Matthew 13:34). Usually, when Jesus was asked a question about abstract concepts, he answered with a story or he used concrete reasoning. Jesus was asked: "Is it lawful to give a poll tax to Caesar or not?" Jesus answered, "Show me the coin used for the poll-tax ..." and then concluded, "Render to Caesar the things that are Caesar's, and to God the things that are God's" (Matthew 22:17-19). A doctor of the Law asked Jesus, "Who is my neighbor?" Jesus answered with the story of the Good Samaritan (Luke 10:25-37).

However, Paul's writings were clearly the language of a well-educated literate communicator. Paul mainly used abstract language, instead of telling stories. Paul translated the gospel written in the storytelling rhetoric of oral communicators into logical reasoning language used by educated literate communicators. He translated ideas expressed in the gospel stories into logical categories of Greek philosophy, in a contextualization effort. Today, preachers whose listeners are preferred oral communicators, including post-literate oral-visual communicators, need to do the opposite of Paul. They need to become storytelling-preachers who take Paul's writings and illustrate them with stories.

The majority of modern listeners are preferred oral-communicators. Post-literates are oral-visual communicators and think in story, not abstract. The preacher, whose text is from the 10% of the Bible that uses logical abstract language, should only preach a biblical truth when he has a story to illustrate it. If a preacher really understands an abstract biblical teaching, no matter how complex it may be, he should be able to illustrate it with a story. The Preaching Cycle will guide the preacher to illustrate biblical truths with stories.

The expository preacher limits himself to his chosen text of Scripture. His job is to make the text understood by his listeners. Every word from the pulpit amplifies, elaborates, illustrates or applies the text at hand. He considers Scripture his authority and limits himself to his text. His goal is for his listeners to understand the text. The Preaching Cycle will guide the preacher to help listeners understand his text.

THE PREACHING CYCLE

The preacher extracts and selects truths from the Scripture text that he wishes to include as his sermon points. Each selected truth becomes a division of the sermon. The preacher should use the **Preaching Cycle** to develop truths chosen to become sermon divisions.

The **Preaching Cycle** requires three activities for each truth selected to become a sermon division:
    1st Explain the truth
    2nd Illustrate the truth
    3rd Apply the truth to listeners' lives

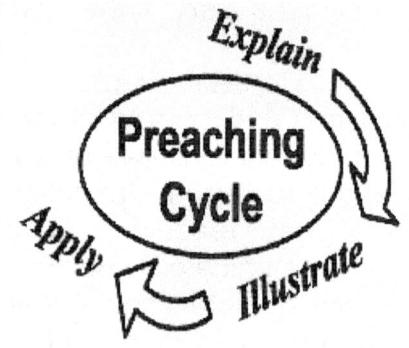

The expository storytelling-preacher develops life-lessons or truths discovered in his text into sermon points. Every spoken word from the pulpit amplifies, elaborates, illustrates, or applies his text. This chapter touches on the three elements in the **Preaching Cycle**. However, most of the chapter's emphasis is on using stories as illustrations, because the thrust of the book is using storytelling in preaching.

1. Explain the truth

The preacher comments on the sermon point, giving facts, details, reasoning, and logic that make clear the truth to his listeners. During explanation--ideas, reasoning, and logic reign. Explanation is analytical in nature. It places a heavy emphasis on the logic of persuasion. It amplifies ideas and gives reasons to prove the idea and to emphasize truth. Explanation explains ideas following the path of reason.

Some of the things the storytelling-preacher does while explaining the truth are:

- Make an idea, situation, or problem clear to listeners by describing it in more detail or revealing relevant facts or ideas.
  Example: Paul states, "Carry each other's burdens, and in this way you will fulfill the law of Christ" (Galatians 6:2 NIV). *Explanation*: This command goes far beyond sympathizing or even empathizing with someone who is experiencing problems or trials that come with life. It means what it says; fellow Christians are to stand shoulder-to-shoulder, side by side, with our brothers and sisters in Christ and endure those burdens with them.
  Example: The Jews in Jesus' day had racial prejudice toward Samaritans. *Explanation*: Samaritans were descendants of Israelites who had intermarried with people who worshiped other gods. The Samaritans tried to worship God and at the same time worship other gods.

- Make something that confuses listeners plain or comprehensible.
  Example: Explain why Mary and Joseph were called husband and wife, even though they were not living

together as husband and wife. Jewish custom considered an engaged couple as husband and wife; even though the ceremony where they would start living together had not taken place.

- Offer rational reasons for the actions, beliefs, or remarks of the Scripture text.
  Example: Immediately after Jesus taught his disciples how to pray, Jesus told them that if they were unwilling to forgive people who wronged them, God the Father would not forgive them (Matthew 6:14-15). *Rational reason*: When a person prays, there is a connection between what God does and what the praying person does. For instance, a person can't get forgiveness from God without also forgiving people who have wronged them. If the praying person refuses to do his part, he cuts himself off from God doing his part. The forgiven person experiences becoming similar to God the Forgiver.

- Restate Scripture teaching by using plain English to paraphrase it.
  Example:
  Life-lesson from Matthew 6:1: The world is not a stage for actors to play the part of being religious. Matthew 6:1 advises us to avoid doing acts of righteousness in a way to be seen by people; because then, God in heaven will not reward us.
  Restating life-lesson by paraphrasing it: This verse advises us to be careful when we are doing good things so that we don't make a performance out of it and call attention to ourselves. It might be good theater; we might be good actors at playing a part. We might get people's applause; however, God won't be applauding.

- Explain the historical and cultural contexts of the text.
  Example: In Galatians 1:7, Paul speaks about some people who were throwing Galatian Christians into confusion and were trying to pervert the gospel of Christ.
  Historical and cultural contexts: Paul planted the church at Galatia when he visited the area and preached the

gospel of the Lord Jesus Christ. After Paul left the region, some Jewish Christians from Jerusalem visited Galatia and insisted that Paul's gospel was incomplete. The Jewish Christians insisted that the complete gospel required non-Jewish men to believe in Jesus Christ, and to accept circumcision; therefore, becoming Jews before they could become Christians.

- Present facts that may not be known, which help listeners understand the truth.
  Example: God told Moses to remove his sandals because he was on Holy Ground. In Egypt, slaves went barefoot. Only non-slaves wore sandals.

- Clarify the reason for emphasizing the life-lesson.
  Example: It is important to emphasize being honest because cheating has become the norm with many Americans who find a way to get free cable television, who make imaginary tax deductions, and who download movies and music from the Internet without paying the fee required.

- Define or clarify words to make them better understood.
  Example: Justification. Justification is God's act of removing the guilt and penalty of sin while at the same time declaring a sinner righteous through Christ's atoning sacrifice on the cross. Righteousness from God is credited to the sinner's account through faith alone, without works.

- Correct misunderstandings. With some Scripture, incorrect understanding has gained popular acceptance and needs to be corrected.
  Example: "However, as it is written: 'What no eye has seen, what no ear has heard, and what no human mind has conceived' —the things God has prepared for those who love him—these are the things God has revealed to us by his Spirit. The Spirit searches all things, even the deep things of God" (1 Corinthians 2:9-10 NIV).
  Misunderstanding corrected: These verses are often applied to the future glory that God has prepared for

believers in Jesus; however, verse 10 makes clear that these are the things that God has now revealed to us believers by his Spirit.

- Clarify what the text does not say.
  Example: The apostle Paul instructs us to "Rejoice in the Lord always. I will say it again: Rejoice!" (Philippians 4:4 NIV). *The text doesn't say*: Notice, Christians are not told to rejoice in all circumstances of life; they are told to always rejoice in the Lord.

- Use logic.
  Logic argues that certain facts fit together in some kind of relationship and that the identified relationship is the correct one. For example, if a white billiard ball hits a red billiard ball, the red ball will move. This statement implies a relation between two billiard balls under certain conditions.
  Example: In 1 Corinthians 15:-12-19, Paul draws logical conclusions against the teaching that there is no resurrection of the dead (15:12). If there is no resurrection, then Jesus Christ didn't rise from the dead. If Christ didn't rise from the dead, preaching is useless. If Christ didn't rise from the dead, faith in Christ is useless (15:14). If Christ didn't rise from the dead, apostles were liars (15:15). If Christ didn't rise from the dead, believers are still in their sins (15:17). If Christ didn't rise from the dead, believers are to be pitied (15:19).

- Use other Bible texts that explain and reinforce the life-lesson.
  The Bible interprets itself. Therefore, the preacher can use parallel texts to explain the Scripture truth being emphasized. Parallel texts are other texts that talk about the same subjects as your text. Parallel texts in Psalms, Proverbs, the Prophets, the teachings of Jesus, Paul's letters, the General Epistles, and Hebrews can be used to explain a scripture truth. Teaching texts, such as the teachings of Jesus and Paul's letters, can be helpful to explain a truth found in a specific text.

Example: Believers in Jesus should forgive one another (Matthew 6:14-15). Immediately after teaching his disciples how to pray, Jesus told them that if they were unwilling to forgive people who wronged them, God the Father would not forgive them (Matthew 6:14-15). Parallel texts: In two different texts, the apostle Paul connects our forgiving others with God forgiving us. 1st Forgive one another, just as God forgives you through Christ (Ephesians 4:31-32). 2nd Forgive one another, just as the Lord forgave you (Colossians 3:12-13).

2. Illustrate the truth

Sermon illustrations are stories which clarify scriptural truths. Stories are spices that give seasoning to expository preaching. The cook can prepare nutritious food without using salt or spices. But few willingly eat the food and gain the nutrition from the food. In the same way, if the preacher expounds on Scripture without including stories that illustrate, most listeners will not digest the truth the preacher sets before them.

A sermon without story-illustrations is like the outside wall of a house without windows. The wall may hold up the roof and keep out the heat or cold, but it doesn't let in light. A house without windows is similar to a prison: dark, oppressive, and uninviting. The root word for window is "wind-door." Before air-conditioning, windows allowed breath of air to refresh a house during hot summer months. A story-illustration both lets in light on the explanation and it allows a breeze of enjoyment to blow over listeners.

Ideas and stories are alternative ways of presenting a Scripture truth. Explanation informs; storytelling creates experiences. During explanation, ideas reign; during illustration, stories reign. During explanation, reasoning and logic reign; during illustration storytelling reigns. Explanation transmits information; storytelling transmits a snapshot of reality. Explanation tells people what to think; a story forces people to think for themselves. A story that illustrates a biblical truth contains a hidden dynamic of living truth that captures attention and furthers understanding in a way that no other sermon tool can match.

Illustrations do not substitute explanation, but they serve to reinforce and confirm it. Illustrations help biblical truths to be understood by emotions and willpower, as well as intellect. Explanation is not superior to story; neither is story superior to explanation. Both are subordinate to Scripture truth. Both are important, because whatever helps communicate God's truth is important. Stories orient people to reality and value. Listeners participate in stories with the physical engagement of their senses.

I suggest that preachers follow this principle: Only preach a biblical truth when you have a story to illustrate it. The preacher should take abstract, obscure, deep and difficult truth, and labor to illustrate it through story. A story should be narrated to illustrate each sermon point.

In the New Testament, Jesus never spoke without telling stories, called parables. The apostle Paul spoke and wrote using the philosophical discourse of the educated. The New Testament has a place for storytelling Jesus and philosophical Paul; the preacher should practice both storytelling and giving interpretative philosophical emphasis. Storytelling was the most formative communication tradition in the religion of Israel. Storytelling was the principal communication tradition of the gospel in New Testament times.

I have included the following story from my book, *PARABLE SEEDS, FIRST SOWING*:
Students were excited to receive a visit from a famous master teacher. They expected the master teacher to expound on deep intellectual truths. However, the teacher told one story after another.
A student requested, "Master, we want to hear you expound on profound philosophical subjects."
The master teacher answered, "The older I get, the more I realize that the shortest road to guide people to the truth is to tell them a story."

Jesus told parables to put his listeners on the road to truth. I encourage preachers to imitate Jesus by also telling stories that will put listeners on the road to truth.

I have a strong conviction that before we preachers can change someone's beliefs, we must change the stories they hear and believe.

Stories use concrete logic. A story, like a nail, can hang up an idea that otherwise would fall to the floor. A good illustration gives listeners a memory hook to recall the sermon point. The preacher needs a story, an anecdote, a joke, or a description of an event that illustrates the truth. A good illustration turns on a light that clarifies the explanation and makes the sermon more interesting for listeners. A story that plays on the listeners' heartstrings will make a point.

Sources for Stories to Illustrate a Biblical Truth

For more information on finding stories to illustrate, see the chapter: ***Where do Stories Come From? Sources for Stories***.

- **Bible stories**. The Bible is the preacher's most important source of stories to tell. The first place the preacher should turn for a story to tell is the Bible. Some preachers refer to an idea gained from a Bible story without telling the story. NO! No! No-no-no-no! Don't just refer to the Bible story. Tell the Bible story.

    The Bible explains itself, and a Bible story is often the best story to illustrate a biblical truth.
    Example: A preacher doing a series of sermons on the Lord's Prayer (Matthew 6:9-13) divided the Lord's Prayer into several petitions. The preacher came to the petition, "Forgive us our debts, as we also have forgiven our debtors" (6:12 NIV). The preacher emphasized, "Forgive us our debts," and told the parable of the Prodigal Son, who asked forgiveness from his earthly father (Luke 15:11-24). When the preacher emphasized, "As we also have forgiven our

debtors," he told the story of the Unmerciful Servant. The servant owed his king a debt he could not pay. The king forgave him much, but the forgiven servant refused to forgive a fellow servant who owed him little (Matthew 18:21-33).

- **Jokes**. If a joke illustrates a biblical truth, include it in the sermon; however, a joke should not be told as a sermon ice-breaker or just to entertain.

- **Anecdotes**. Anecdotes are very short stories that make a point. _Example_: A contractor refused to build a home for a young couple. He told them, "Your house plans have the windows too high. I'll not build a house with windows so high that children can't see out."

- **Comparisons**. A comparison shows how one thing or person is similar to another. It examines two or more items to establish similarities and dissimilarities. _Example_: A story is like a nail. It can hold something up that would fall to the floor.

- **Analogy**. An analogy shows similarity in some respect between things that are otherwise dissimilar. The preacher can take a doctrinal truth and explain it in terms grounded in life, proceeding from the known to the unknown. _Example_: Jesus used analogy in the parable of the sower to set forth the four types of responses people give to the teaching/preaching of God's Word.

- **Other people's stories**. Find stories from the lives of other people that illustrate biblical truth. Weave other people's personal experiences into sermons to illustrate biblical truth. _Caution_: Never betray confidences when telling another person's story.

- **Significant life events**. Significant life-events are full of stories that illustrate biblical truth.
Examples of significant life-events: Starting school, birthdays, holidays, family reunions, moving, graduating,

getting married, death of a loved one, an accident or sickness of a family member are all significant life events.

- **Sports events**. Sports are full of human events and conflicts. Conflict is an essential part of stories and sports are all about people competing. Sports fans always pay attention when a story from sports is used to illustrate biblical teachings.

- **Historical events**. History has a way of repeating itself. Issues dealt with in stories about people from the past are still relevant for today's listeners.

- **Contemporary events**. Most of the news is presented in story form and many news stories are useful to illustrate biblical teaching. The storytelling-preacher will find many stories if he watches the news or reads it regularly.

- **Literature**. In literature, the storytelling-preacher finds stories written by someone else for the purpose of publication. Remember to respect copyright laws and name the author and where it was published when telling a published story. Literature can also help the preacher with seed-ideas for crafting original stories.

- **World of art**. Wonderful stories can be discovered from novels, movies, drama, popular songs, and television. Expressions of culture reveal to us the world-view of our time. Popular works of art are popular because they give voice to what many people are feeling and thinking. The preacher who illustrates with works of art will share a story that is relevant to his listeners' lives.

- **Craft your own stories**. Sometimes the preacher knows the kind of story he needs to tell, but cannot find one from any other source, so he crafts his own story. Many will argue that crafting a story is a work of art which few can master. I teach storytelling and have the conviction that most people are natural born storytellers who lost the art of storytelling in school. The adult who is willing to let the little child within him come out and play will rediscover his storytelling skills.

Cautions to Take with Story-Illustrations

- <u>Do not tell stories in a sermon just to entertain</u>. Do not tell stories just to make things more interesting, or to give listeners something to laugh about. Illustrations are a means, not an end. The goal of a sermon is to communicate biblical truths. Include stories in a sermon to make the Bible come alive, to enlighten Scripture, and help listeners hear the greatest story every told.

- <u>Make sure the story illustrates the sermon point</u>. Stories, jokes, examples, and anecdotes that do not clarify or support the biblical truth of the sermon point become weak elements in the sermon. Likewise, stories just entertain when they don't clarify the truth being presented. <u>Caution</u>: A good story that the preacher heard or read may become pushy and arrogant, demanding to be told in next Sunday's sermon, whether it belongs there or not.

- <u>Avoid giving away the point of a story in the introduction</u>. Don't tell what the story is about before telling it. Don't introduce a story with something like, "I'm going to tell you a story that warns you about the harm of greed," or "I'm going to tell you a story about a man who learned to be thankful in difficult times." Listeners are not inspired to hear a story if they already know the point or its thrust.

- <u>Seek illustrations from a variety of sources</u>. Don't overload the sermon with illustrations about the same subject. Sermons need stories from a variety of sources and on a variety of subjects. <u>Example of what not to do</u>: One preacher is an avid fan of the Dallas Cowboys and every sermon he preaches has Dallas Cowboys stories, and most all his illustrations are about football. Don't ride a hobby-horse by always telling stories about a special interest, whether geology, your hobby, sports, hunting, fishing, your family, or politics. Use a variety of sources.

- The length of a story is not the test of its effectiveness. The test is: Does it let in light? Some of Jesus' illustrations were very short. *Example*: Jesus called his disciples "the light of the world" and "the salt of the earth" (Matthew 5:14-16). *A modern example*: "Worrying about the future is like taking a trip with the car's emergency brake on."

    A good story, that illustrates a biblical truth, may be short and simple. Take time to simplify stories used for illustrations. Most illustrations should take less than a minute to tell. Some stories can be told in less than 15 seconds. Nothing kills an illustration like unnecessary length. Avoid dragging out illustrations by giving unnecessary information or going off in tangents.

- Avoid stories about things listeners know nothing about. Listeners can only understand illustrations that relate to their experiences. I was raised on a farm in Alabama during a time when "Cotton was King." Stories about my hoeing and picking cotton don't communicate to people who were raised in a city. I grew up playing baseball; however, I moved to Brazil where "Soccer is King" and I found illustrations about soccer instead of baseball. It's difficult for Brazilians living in equatorial jungles to understand an illustration about children having a snowball fight.

- Be honest. Don't tell an embellished story or a camouflaged one as a true story. Do not palm off fiction as fact. Do not tell a story that happened to another person as though it happened to you. Don't claim you crafted a story you heard someone else tell, or you found in a book, or on the internet. Tell listeners when you are telling a fictional story. Introduce the camouflaged story with something similar to: "This may not be a true story; however, it does illustrate truth," or "This fictional story happens to people every day," or "I can't vouch for the truth of the following story." Listeners will not believe a preacher is preaching the truth if they catch him lying.

- Check the facts before stating that something is true in a story. While writing this chapter, I was preparing to tell a story about the origin of the melody "Taps." I read from several sources that the melody was found in the pocket of a dead Confederate soldier during the Civil War by the boy's own father who was a Union officer. I checked "snopes.com" and discovered that the story is false. Many untrue stories spread without factual foundations, then gain credence through repetition. When telling a story as truth, exercise care to tell it without exaggeration or embellishment. Check your facts, and if you have doubts about the truthfulness of facts within your story, say something like, "I can't vouch for the truthfulness of this story." Listeners are often better informed about many subjects than the preacher. If knowledgeable people hear a preacher make a factual error in a story, they may wonder, "If the preacher doesn't have his facts straight about earthly items, can I trust him when he talks of spiritual matters?"

- <u>Don't betray confidences</u>. Do not use the story of a person in the congregation without getting that person's permission. And before telling the story, state that the person gave you permission to tell it. Never-never-ever tell stories from the pulpit that come from the pastor's counseling ministry without permission. Preachers who illustrate with counseling experiences will discover that church members are reluctant to seek counsel from a pastor who is likely to turn their case into sermon illustrations.

- <u>Avoid too much "I."</u> The preacher should avoid calling more attention to himself than to the Bible. It is good to share personal experiences; however, the preacher needs to avoid coming across as bragging. He should not make himself the hero of every story he tells. He should avoid name-dropping. It is helpful for listeners if the preacher tells stories about himself as the fall guy or the one who makes mistakes.

- <u>Some stories need to be camouflaged and told as fiction</u>. Some stories beg to be told; however, people in the story need to stay anonymous. Some people's stories deal with issues that should never be shared in public. Some people's stories would embarrass them or create problems for them in the future. I follow the practice of naming the hero who did good, and camouflaging the villain who did evil or the person who put himself in an embarrassing situation. If I receive a story-idea from people who need to remain anonymous, I camouflage the incident, reinvent story-characters, situations, locations, and tell the story as fiction. I seek to camouflage the story so much that original characters would not recognize themselves in the story.

- <u>Don't overload a sermon point with too many illustrations</u>. Select the best stories to illustrate the desired biblical truth. Don't use every story you find on a point. Illustrations, like windows, let in light. If a room has plenty of light, and you put in more windows, the room's occupants may be blinded with the glare.

- <u>Don't allow an illustration to overshadow the biblical truth</u>. A story told in a sermon should not call attention to itself, but should throw light on the sermon point.

- <u>A well-selected story does not need to be explained</u>. The preacher does not need to explain how the story illustrates the biblical truth. Let the story do its work. Follow the example of Jesus who seldom explained his parables. Most of the time he followed his parable-story with the statement, "He who has ears, let him hear."

3. Apply the truth to listeners' lives

An application establishes what God desires the listeners to know, to be, or to do as a result of understanding a truth understood from Scripture. Applications show how the listeners should put the truth to use in their own lives. Applications explain what listeners need to do or how they need to change in order to practice the truth communicated from Scripture.

Three types of applications:
1st <u>Personal application</u>: a biblical truth applied to oneself. The preacher should apply the Scripture to his own life before he applies it to other people. Don't ask others to deal with an issue until you have dealt with the same issue. *Example*: A preacher who doesn't tithe should start tithing before he challenges others to tithe. *Example*: A preacher who is tempted to look at porn on

his computer should make sure he is avoiding porn before he challenges others to resist the temptation to watch porn. *Example*: A preacher shared the following example: "I need to love those teenagers who throw beer cans on my lawn every weekend. I need to greet them with a smile during the week, and pray for God to bless them when I'm picking up the beer cans early Sunday morning.

2nd <u>General application</u>: one that is external and serves for all people in all locations at all times in history. *Example*: "We need to love one another."

3rd <u>Specific ecclesiastical or external application</u>: one that applies biblical teaching to specific people or a local church. *Example*: "Our church needs to show love for the immigrants who live in our community by starting a literacy class, teaching them English as a second language."

All truths presented in a sermon should have as a common goal: to get listeners to change! The preacher should desire that listeners' lives be transformed as a result of his preaching. The change may be emotional, intellectual, behavioral, physical or a combination of all four, but it must occur for the sermon to be successful. The preacher wants his listeners to change in one or more of the following ways:

- Believe a truth they haven't believed
- Trust a promise they haven't trusted
- Understand a truth they haven't understood
- Obey a command or law they haven't been obeying
- Become something they haven't been
- Do something they haven't been doing

Application may require instruction. The preacher should not send listeners away convinced they should obey a specific Bible teaching and longing to do it without knowing how. *Example*: The preacher who challenges his listeners to share the good news of Jesus to non-believers needs to instruct them on how to share the Gospel. *Example*: The preacher who challenges his listeners to daily read the Bible and pray, needs to instruct them how to read the Bible and how to pray.

Application explains how the listeners should change by putting the truths presented into action. Appeal for the listeners to apply the truth presented to their own lives. Clarify how the listeners should change and make an appeal for them to change.

CONCLUSION TO PREACHING CYCLE

The **Preaching Cycle** touches the listener's:
- Brain (explanation)
- Heart (stories that illustrate)
- Personal life (application)

The preacher who touches all three elements of the **Preaching Cycle** in a rhythm that explains, illustrates and applies will keep his listeners tuned in to his sermon.

This chapter explained the **Preaching Cycle**; however, the main emphasis is on illustrations, since the thrust of this book is using storytelling in preaching.

Worksheet: SERMON OUTLINE FOR NON-STORY TEXT

Introduction: Catch Fire with First Sentence
(*Story-appetizer, to catch fire with first sentence.*)
Bridge-building paragraph from fire-catching opening statement or story to Scripture-text

Sermon Divisions, Utilizing the Preaching Cycle

1. 1st Sermon Division (1st Life-lesson from text to be preached)
   Explanation:

   Illustration:

   Application:

2. 2nd Sermon Division (2nd Life-lesson from text to be preached)
   Explanation:

   Illustration:

   Application:

3. 3rd Sermon Division (3rd Life-lesson from text to be preached)
   Explanation:

   Illustration:

   Application:

CONCLUSION
   1st Summarize:
   - Principal facts of text
   - Life-lessons (divisions of the sermon) treated

   2nd Invite listeners to change by putting truths and applications presented into action

EXAMPLE: *Sermon on Non-Story Text with Story-Appetizer and Story-Illustrations*

EVIDENCE OF LOVING GOD
1 John 4:19 – 5:5

Story-appetizer: **BIBLE DIDN'T HELP DOG EXPRESS LOVE FOR GOD**

When Tim, our youngest son, was three years old, we had a fenced in yard. I bought a Doberman Pincher puppy that we named Prince. Our two oldest sons went to school during the day and Tim played outside with his dog Prince.

Prince became protective of Tim. We, his parents, could not discipline Tim in the yard. If we raised our voice when speaking to Tim, Prince got between Tim and us. If Tim cried, Prince got between Tim and us, and showed his teeth. If children came to play with Tim, we had to lock up Prince because the dog would attack Tim's playmates.

A year passed. Tim was four years old and Prince was one year old. Tim loved to imitate people. Every Sunday when we came home from church, Doris started lunch and Tim went into my study to get a New Testament. Then Tim went to the backyard and preached to Prince. Tim imitated the gestures and voice of our pastor. He held the New Testament in his hand just like the pastor held his Bible. Once, a pastor who walked with a limp preached at our church. That Sunday, Tim walked with a limp as he preached to Prince.

One Sunday, Tim observed his oldest brother Sam being baptized by immersion at the Baptist church. We returned home and Tim went into the backyard, filled a bucket with water and poured it over Prince. Tim wasn't satisfied with Prince's baptism; so he filled up the bucket again with water and chased the elusive dog around the backyard.

A couple of Sundays, Doris called Tim to enter the house for lunch and Tim forgot his New Testament in the backyard. Prince chewed up and swallowed each New Testament.

Prince heard the Bible preached every Sunday. He fed on the Bible. He was baptized; however, he grew meaner toward people who were not part of our family. Weekly listening to preaching, being baptized, and feeding on the Word of God didn't change Prince. Prince continued to manifest his dog nature.

Bridge Paragraph:

The dog Prince gave no evidence that he loved God. It's easy to say we love God, if that love doesn't cost us anything more than spoken words and church attendance. Our text for today gives a combination of three tests that give evidence that a person loves God. The love for God has three inescapable consequences: love of God's children; obedience to God; victory over the world.

Read 1 John 4:19 – 5:5.

1. Belief in Jesus Makes a Person a Child of God
(1 John 5:1)

Explanation:

A person is born into God's family when he believes Jesus is the Christ (1 John 5:1). He believes that the Old Testament promises of the Coming One were fulfilled in Jesus. He believes that Jesus is who he claimed to be. He believes that Jesus is the Son of God and is equal to God the Father. He believes that Jesus was crucified and arose from the grave.

All who believe in Jesus become God's children. "Yet to all who received him, to those who believed in his name, he gave the right to become children of God—children born not of natural descent, not of human decision or a husband's will, but born of God" (John 1:12-13 NIV).

Illustration:

A person could only become a child of my wife and I by one of two ways. My wife could become pregnant and give birth to the person, or we could adopt the person.

Application:

A person can only become a child of God by one way. He believes that Jesus Christ is the Son of God, who lived a sinless life, but was rejected by people who crucified him. While God allowed sinful people to crucify his Son, God raised Jesus from the dead.

2. Love of God the Father Is Evidenced by Loving God's Children (1 John 4:20-21)

Explanation:

When a person becomes a believer in Jesus, he becomes a child of God and part of God's family. Two people who have the same father are siblings. Fellow believers in Jesus are brothers and sisters. God determines who family members are, not individual believers.

Each believer has the duty to accept and love all whom God accepts into his family. Anyone who fails to love his bother and sister who he can see, can't love God the Father whom he has not seen (1 John 4:20-21). This text combines two actions that always walk hand in hand: love God – love God's children. Love all God's children, no exceptions. Love of God and love of other people can't be separated. Anyone who professes to love God while he hates fellow Christians is deluded; his profession is a lie. Love for God and hatred for brothers and sisters in Christ can't coexist in the same heart. Love of God expresses itself in a loving concern for fellow Christians.

An expert in the law of Moses was trying to trap Jesus and asked him a question, "Teacher, which is the greatest commandment in the law?"

Jesus answered, "Love the Lord your God with all your heart, your soul, and your mind. This is the first and greatest commandment. The second greatest commandment is similar to it: Love your neighbor as yourself. All of Moses' teachings and the prophets hang on these two commandments" (Matthew 22:34-40).

The apostle Paul repeated Jesus teaching, saying, "The commandments, 'Do not commit adultery,' 'Do not murder,' 'Do not steal,' 'Do not covet,' and whatever other commandment there may be, are summed up in this one rule: 'Love your neighbor as yourself.' Love does no harm to its neighbor. Therefore, love is the fulfillment of the law" (Romans 13:9-10 NIV).

Illustrations:

A single parent would not be impressed by a date who said, "I love you but I can't stand your children."

An old, old story is set in the time when children walked or rode horses to school. A stranger saw a boy carrying a younger brother on his back; it was obvious the younger boy was lame; he couldn't walk. The stranger asked, "Are you carrying your brother to school?"
The boy answered, "Yes."
The stranger said, "He must be a heavy burden for you to carry!"
The boy answered, "He ain't heavy; he's my brother."

Jesus gave practical examples of what love is when he posed the following story pertaining to the final judgment, saying, "Then the King will say to those on his right, 'Come, you who are blessed by my Father; take your inheritance, the kingdom prepared for you since the creation of the world. For I was hungry and you gave me something to eat, I was thirsty and you gave me something to drink, I was a stranger and you invited me in, I needed clothes and you clothed me, I was sick and you looked after me, I was in prison and you came to visit me.'
"Then the righteous will answer him, 'Lord, when did we see you hungry and feed you, or thirsty and give you something to drink? When did we see you a stranger and invite you in, or needing clothes and clothe you? When did we see you sick or in prison and go to visit you?'
"The King will reply, 'Truly I tell you, whatever you did for one of the least of these brothers and sisters of mine, you did for me'" (Matthew 25:34-40 NIV).

Application:

It's easy to say we love God, if that love doesn't cost us anything more than spoken words and church attendance. But, the real test of our love for God is how we treat people – God's family members who are our fellow believers. Anyone who is a child of God is our brother or sister. We give evidence that we love God by expressing our love for our brothers and sisters in Christ. We give evidence that we love God when we help fellow believers in need to deal with their problems.

3. Love of God the Father Is Evidenced by Obeying God's Commands (1 John 5:3)

Explanation:

Our text combines loving God and keeping his commandments. "This is love for God: to obey his commands. And his commands are not burdensome" (1 John 5:3 NIV). Love seeks to please the one who is loved.

Examples of a few commandments given by God are the following: believe in Jesus; confess sins; be baptized; observe the Lord's supper; don't neglect the meeting together of believers; pray; pray for God to bless those who mistreat you; forgive others as you want God to forgive you; continue in faith; make disciples. A person gives evidence that he loves God by obeying God's commands (1 John 5:2).

The Holy Spirit guides believers to know God's will for their lives. A Christian who reads the Bible and prays for God's leadership may receive an urging from the Holy Spirit to do something for God. The Holy Spirit can give God's commands to individuals, informing them of his will for their lives.

The believer in Jesus has freedom to choose to do wrong or to do right; to obey God or to disobey. The Christian doesn't lose his human nature that gives him ability to disobey God. If he did, he would cease to be human and would become a machine. The Christian has the choice to allow the Holy Spirit freedom to posses him and deliver him from sin, guide him to make right decisions, and to express love for God by obeying his commands. But evidence that a person loves God is seen when he obeys God's commands.

God's commandments are not a burden to the person who loves him (1 John 5:3). Jesus never promised that obeying his commands would be easy. But, the hard work and self-discipline required to obey him is not a burden. It may be difficult, but it's not a burden.

Illustration:

Jesus invited potential followers, "Take my yoke upon you and learn from me, for I am gentle and humble in heart, and you will find rest for your souls. For my yoke is easy and my burden is light" (Matthew 11:29-30 NIV). A yoke was made to fit an animal in order to enable it to pull a heavy load. A well-made yoke would perfectly fit an animal; it would not rub his neck and create sores and blisters. The animal with a well-made yoke could pull a heavy load without it becoming a burden. Jesus accused the Scribes and Pharisees of binding heavy burdens that were hard to bear and placing them on people's shoulders (Matthew 23:4). The mass of rules and regulations became an intolerable burden on anyone who tried to keep them.

Sometimes, it was hard for my wife and I to live in Brazil as missionaries for thirty-three years. It was hard for me to learn Portuguese. It was hard when each son graduated from high school and flew to the USA to do university studies. However, our missionary work was the hardest job we ever loved. We felt like we were doing what we were born to do.

I crafted the following story, "**It's a Mockingbird**." It's not a true story, but it does illustrate true life.

The sixty year old daughter visited her eighty-four year old mother, who had fallen. The daughter came to help for a couple of weeks while the mother recovered from a fall and regained her strength, so that she could walk around without a walker.

The two were in the living room. The mother was sitting in her granny rocking chair reading a book, while the daughter reclined in a lazy boy recliner reading a book on her iPad.

Suddenly, a slender bodied gray bird landed on the windowsill behind the mother and belted out an endless string of more than ten different bird sounds.

The mother asked, "What was that?"

The daughter answered, "That was a Mockingbird, mimicking the songs of several different birds."

After a couple of minutes of silence, again the bird loudly and in rapid succession belted out the sounds of different birds.

The mother asked, "What was that?"

The daughter replied, "Mother, I just told you; it's a Mockingbird."

Meanwhile, the Mockingbird was conspicuous as it ran and hopped along the windowsill. It again made its presence known to the two ladies inside the room by belting out an endless string of several different bird sounds.

The mother asked, "What was that?"

The daughter raised her voice, "Mother, it's a Mockingbird; it's a Mockingbird!"

After a couple of minutes of silence, the Mockingbird belted out another endless string of several different bird sounds.

The mother asked, "What was that?"

The daughter screamed with irritation, "Mother, I've told you a dozen times, 'It's a Mockingbird!' Can't you remember? It's a Mockingbird! It's a Mockingbird!"

The mother grabbed her walker, pulled herself up, and made her way to her bedroom. The mother returned to the living room with several old diaries. She started keeping diaries when she was a teenager. After a half hour of looking through different diaries, the mother handed one opened diary to her daughter and said, "Read this."

The daughter read the following words in her mother's old diary, "Today was the first warm spring day after a bitter cold winter. Birds returned to our yard after a winter of absence. My three year old daughter napped and I sat in my rocking chair in front of a window to read. I'd only read a few pages when my little girl came into the room and interrupted my reading by climbing onto my lap. She cuddled against me and laid still; so I continued my reading.

"Suddenly a slender bodied gray Mockingbird landed on the windowsill behind me. The Mockingbird belted out an endless string of several different bird sounds.

"My daughter asked, 'Mommy, what was that?'

"I answered, 'That was a Mockingbird, mimicking the songs of several different birds.'

"My daughter again nested against my breast and the Mockingbird belted out another string of several different bird sounds. My daughter sat up so fast that she knocked my book to the floor. She asked, 'What was that?'

"I again answered, 'It's a Mockingbird, mimicking the songs of several different birds.'

"At first I was irritated that my daughter kept asking me, 'What was that?' Then I realized that this was a precious moment as I held her in my arms and she cuddled against me. We kept sitting and I counted; she asked me sixteen different times, 'What was that?' And each time I answered, 'It's a Mockingbird, mimicking the songs of several different birds.'"

It was difficult for the mother of a young child to find time to sit down, rest, and read. It was hard for the young mother when she put her young daughter down for a nap and sat down to read, but her child didn't want to sleep; she wanted to sit in her mother's lap. Although it was difficult, the young mother did not consider the child she loved as a burden.

Application:
It's easy to say we love God, if that love doesn't cost us anything more than spoken words and church attendance. But, the real test of our love for God is how we treat people—God's family members who are our fellow believers, and how we obey God's commands.

The Holy Spirit living within us makes it possible for us to do anything God asks us to do. When we love God, we want to please him. We give evidence that we love God by obeying his commands. Some of God's commands are demanding, but when we love God, his commands are not a burden.

4. Love of God the Father Is Evidenced by Experiencing Victory Over the World (1 John 5:4-5)

Explanation:
Not only does the believer in Jesus give evidence that he loves God, the believer experiences overcoming the world. "...For everyone born of God overcomes the world. This is the victory that has overcome the world, even our faith. Who is it that overcomes the world? Only he who believes that Jesus is the Son of God" (1 John 5:4-5). Faith in Jesus Christ overcomes the world. Faith in Jesus results in a new birth – birth into the family of God. Being born into the family of God is a supernatural experience which takes a person out of the spear of the world where Satan rules and into the family of God. It is not the person

who conquers the world; it's faith in Jesus that conquers the world. Faith in Jesus gives victory. When a person first puts his faith in Jesus, the Son of God, he has initial victory over the world. The world's hold on him is broken. Faith births a person into God's family and gives him power to continually experience victory.

The Bible often uses the word "world" to refer collectively to all people on earth who are estranged from God, and who are a part of the world system that is in conflict with the Kingdom of God. The world gives importance to things that will pass away. It craves satisfying the desires of the sinful nature, obtaining possessions that can be seen, and boasting of things of this life (1 John 2:15-17).

Victory is not the assurance that the believer will come out on top, nor that he will win every contest, nor that he will always have good health, nor that his loved ones will always recover from sickness, nor that he will be wealthy, nor that he will be rewarded for being honest. Victory is resisting temptation that would bring instant pleasure but would disobey God. Victory is taking a stand for right when the majority takes a stand for wrong. Victory is speaking the truth to people who reject the truth. Victory is making the right choice when it costs you. Victory is becoming more like Jesus in places where Jesus isn't popular.

Illustration:
An accountant once told me, "I can't afford to become an honest Christian. If I become honest, my CEO would accuse me of working for the government instead of working for the company." The accountant did confess his belief in Jesus. The accountant told his CEO that he would no longer cook the books, and the CEO asked him to resign. It took the accountant six years to regain the income he had when he first became a Christian and lost his job. The accountant was victorious over the world system that encouraged him to be dishonest in order to have more money and things that money would buy.

Application:
Believers in Jesus have assurance of final victory over the world. We can experience present victory. Faith in Jesus

combined with love for God enables us to have victory when we are the only ones who take a stand for doing right. Faith in Jesus and love for God enable us to have victory when we resist temptation that would bring instant pleasure but would disobey God. Faith in Jesus and love for God enable us to have victory when we make the right choices that costs us. Faith in Jesus and love for God enable us to have victory when we become more like Jesus in places where Jesus isn't popular.

CONCLUSION:

It's easy to identify a neighbor as an officer of the law when he arrives home with his uniform, badge, and gun on his belt. But, it is not obvious that he is an officer of the law when he's wearing Bermuda shorts and a tee shirt, working in his front yard.

1. Become a child of God by believing in Jesus Christ, the Son of God, who died on the cross and arose from the grave.

2. Our text describes the three tests that combine together to identify us as people who love God. If you are failing one of these tests, make a decision to make the changes that will enable you to pass these tests and give evidence that you love God.
    2.1 Give evidence that you love God by loving each and every fellow believer. Show your love by helping fellow believers who are in need.
    2.2 Give evidence that you love God by obeying God's commands – commands found in the Bible, and guidance that comes from the Spirit of God.
    2.3 Give evidence that you love God and have faith in Jesus by experiencing victory over this world that is in conflict with the Kingdom of God.

DESSERT FOR BIBLE STORY-LISTENERS
Embellished Bible Stories

In Western culture, dessert is a course that typically comes at the end of a meal. Its taste is usually sweet. The word comes from Old French *desservir*, meaning "to clear the table." Common desserts include cakes, cookies, fruits, pastries, ice cream, and candies.

Desserts taste better than nutritious food. Most children prefer to skip nutritious vegetables and only eat desserts. However, if a person only eats desserts, he will not have a balanced diet and will become sickly.

In my opinion, embellished Bible stories should be considered the desserts of Bible storytelling. The truth is, most listeners prefer embellished Bible stories over the stories found in the Bible. But, if listeners have a steady diet of embellished stories, they will not be spiritually balanced.

Desserts should be served after a nutritious meal. Embellished Bible stories should only be told to people who have been fed the nutritious story that is found in the Bible.

Many beginning Bible storytellers start telling embellished stories. Listeners like the embellished stories so much, that some storytellers never learn to tell Bible stories as they are narrated in the Bible. In an age when fewer people read, the embellished story may be the only version that the listeners hear. Listeners who only know the embellished story don't know the true Bible story.

Peter advised his listeners to desire God's pure word just like babies desire milk (1 Peter 2:2). Mothers wouldn't give their babies contaminated milk, and storytellers should be cautious not to give listeners contaminated Bible stories.

There are four levels of accuracy in telling Bible stories. (*The story of Jesus in Martha and Mary's home (Luke 10:38-42) is used to illustrate the levels of accuracy.*)

1st **Provable** – The events or facts can be proved by the Bible narrative or historical facts outside the Bible. *Example*: When Jesus came to the sisters' home, Martha was busy with many details and Mary sat at the feet of Jesus listening.

2nd **Probable** – It is likely, but not certain the events happened or the facts are true. *Example*: Martha was a widow. Her husband had died of leprosy. John 12:1-3 records Mary pouring perfume on Jesus at a dinner in Bethany. Matthew 26:6-9 describes the same incident and said it took place in the home of Simon, who had suffered from leprosy. So it is probable that Martha had been married to Simon and was now a widow.

3rd **Possible** – Something that could have happened or could be true, but there is no evidence to prove it. *Example*: Jesus surprised Martha and Mary with a visit. Martha became busy straightening up the house and preparing lunch for Jesus.

4th **Embellished** – Imagination is used to invent events and details beyond those recorded in the Bible. *Example*: Martha went to the village market to buy food, as was her custom every week. Martha was surprised to discover Jesus and his disciples buying food at the market. Martha invited Jesus to come to their house for something to eat. Jesus accepted, said he'd bring the disciples along, and accompanied Martha back home.

I seldom tell embellished Bible stories. I usually only include in my stories events, details, and dialogues that are probable from the Bible text or some historical source. I encourage those I train to stick to provable facts found in the Bible or history when telling a Bible story. However, I'm aware that embellished stories are popular with many storytellers and listeners. I give this counsel: Only tell embellished Bible stories to listeners who know the story accurately as it is recorded in the Bible.

If you desire to embellish a story to listeners with limited Bible knowledge, be sure to tell the Bible version first. Then tell the embellished version. Just as you would not serve children desserts before meat and vegetables, tell the true Bible story before telling the embellished story.

Many preachers assume their listeners are familiar with the Bible. However, many of today's listeners don't know Bible stories.

I have a friend named Fred. One Sunday, Fred was sitting in Sunday School when a church leader called him out of the class and said, "The youth teacher is sick and we need you to teach the youth class."

Fred was not prepared to teach. He decided to play some games with the youth. He said, "There were two men named Saul in the Bible. One was a king, another became an apostle. Whose story is in the Old Testament and whose is in the New?"

The students struggled to guess the correct answer. Fred asked another question, "I'm a wee little man. I climbed a tree to see an important man. What's my name and who did I want to see?"

The students didn't know the answer. Most of those youth had grown up attending church from the time they were babies. If those church-going youth were unfamiliar with Bible stories, the preacher should realize that many of his listeners don't know Bible stories.

My son Sam is also a storyteller. Once he was telling stories to a group of high school students. He asked how many had heard the story of David and Goliath. About 40% raised their hands. Sixty percent said they had never heard the story of David and Goliath. Those sixty percent would be unable to distinguish between an embellished story and a factual Bible story. The storytelling-preacher should assume that most of his listeners are unfamiliar with Bible stories.

My conviction is: If a storyteller embellishes a Bible story to listeners who are unfamiliar with the Bible story, he gives them a contaminated version of the Bible. A diet of embellished Bible stories to listeners without knowledge of the true Bible story will give them biblical misinformation.

Another consideration: People may have a biblical foundation, but if time has passed since they heard a story, their memory may have faded and they may not discern between the factual biblical story and an embellished one. Stories not repeated tend to fade from memory; therefore, Bible stories need to be repeated to refresh memories.

Once I told the story of Joseph in Potiphar's house (Genesis 39). A listener said that Potiphar's wife had her eye on Joseph before Potiphar bought him. I replied that the Bible doesn't teach that. My listener told me how another preacher-storyteller had narrated the story, "Mr. and Mrs. Potiphar went together to the slave market. Mrs. Potiphar noticed Joseph, the young muscular Hebrew. She thought, 'Wow, I bet he could satisfy my cravings in bed. It would be great to have him at home when my Mr. Potiphar is away at work.'
"Mrs. Potiphar told her husband, 'Honey, that one is young and strong. He could do a hard day's work. He'll be a good investment. Why don't you buy him.'
"As soon as Mr. Potiphar's brought Joseph home, Mrs. Potiphar began to connive to get Mr. Potiphar to assign Joseph to work inside their home."

This embellished version disagrees with the biblical version. The Bible states that Potiphar put Joseph in charge of his household only after he noticed that God gave Joseph success in everything he did (Genesis 39:3-4). The Bible says that it was after Joseph was in charge of Potiphar's household that Potiphar's wife noticed him and desired to go to bed with him (Genesis 39:7).

I had the joy of hearing a storytelling-pastor faithfully tell the story of Jonah. He finished the story and asked his listeners, "What most impressed you about the story?"

A listener replied, "I heard a preacher tell the story in a way that explains why the people at Nineveh believed Jonah's message. The people in Nineveh listened to Jonah because of the sailors' testimonies. The sailors arrived at the port before Jonah. The ship stopped at every port and the ship arrived in Nineveh just before Jonah. The sailors were telling everyone about the storm, how they threw Jonah into the sea, how a big fish swallowed him, and then the sea calmed. Just when they finished their story, Jonah appeared, covered with seaweed and fish vomit. The sailors pointed to Jonah and shouted, 'There's the man we're talking about.' The crowd ran to Jonah and crowded around him. Jonah shouted to the gathered crowd, 'In forty days, Nineveh will be destroyed.' The people believed Jonah because of the sailors' testimonies."

But the Bible story disagrees with the embellished story. The Bible doesn't mention the sailors' testimonies. The Bible states that the ship and sailors were headed for Tarshish, which is in the opposite direction from Nineveh (Jonah 1:3).

The leader of a Bible Story Home Study Group told about a young lady who kept coming up with weird interpretations of Bible stories. The leader discovered that the young mother had a collection of all the Veggie Tales Bible story films. She had watched these films with her children. But, she had not read these stories in the Bible. As a result, her understanding of the Bible stories was distorted.

There is the danger that embellished Bible stories give listeners biblical misinformation. If you choose to embellish a Bible story, first make sure your listeners know the story as found in the Bible, and you need to inform them that you used your imagination to embellish the story.

EXAMPLES OF EMBELLISHED BIBLE STORIES

I'm including three examples of embellished Bible stories.

Example # 1: **THE SAPLING OAK**
(Exodus 2:11-15 Embellished)

An angry forty-year old man murdered a cruel government official. The murderer fled from the police to a foreign country where he couldn't be extradited and sentenced to death. The murderer's escape route took him across rocky, dry wasteland. He spotted a cluster of trees in the dry country and realized, "There's a spring with drinking water!"

Near the spring, under a large oak tree, the murderer spotted a young sapling oak tree. He cut the sapling tree to use as a walking pole to aid him as he hiked the rocky terrain.

That's how Moses got his staff that God later used to perform great miracles.

Example # 2: **JESUS IN THE HOME OF MARTHA AND MARY** (Luke 10:38-42 Embellished)

Two single sisters, Martha and Mary, lived together in the village of Bethany. Martha was a widow; her husband had died of leprosy. Mary was the youngest and had yet to marry.

One day Martha told Mary, "I'll go to the village market and buy food; you straighten up the house."
Mary answered, "I'll straighten the house after I say my prayers in the garden."
Martha replied, "You spend too much time in the garden. Make sure the house is in order."
Mary answered, "The house is in order. You mopped the floors yesterday."
Martha wiped a rag across the door frame and said, "Look, Mary, there's dust above the door and window frames."
Mary answered, "Martha, there's more to life than a spotless house!"

Martha saw Jesus at the market. Jesus made his way toward her. Martha said, "Jesus, so good to see you again. I didn't know you were in the village."

Jesus answered, "I've just arrived."

Martha insisted, "Jesus, you must come by the house. We enjoyed your last visit so much."

Jesus answered, "I enjoyed it too. Tell you what. I'll be there in a couple of hours. This time I'll bring the boys."

Martha answered, "Oh, that's great. We'll look forward to your visit."

However, Martha was thinking, "Oh, no! I only meant to invite Jesus. Those aren't boys traveling with Jesus; those are twelve grown men. I've got to hurry and fix a meal for thirteen men. Oh, no! I bet Mary is still in the garden enjoying the flowers and watching the birds. I'll remind her to get the house ready before I finish my shopping."

Martha rushed home and found Mary in the garden looking at flowers. Martha shouted, "Mary, Jesus is in town."

Mary shouted, "That's marvelous. I'll get my shawl and let's go see him."

Martha said, "Mary, you've got work to do. Jesus is coming here. Mary, you've got to get the house spotless. He'll be here in a couple of hours. He's bringing his disciples. We've got to prepare a meal for thirteen men!"

Mary said, "Let's fix sandwiches. That'll give us more time to visit with him."

Martha replied, "Mary, it's Jesus! We've got to fix a meal worthy of Jesus. Now, you build a fire for cooking and clean up the house. I'll buy the food. Mary, you do know how to use a broom?"

Mary answered, "Yes, Martha, I know how to use a broom!"

Martha answered, "Then sweep the house and build the fire. I'll buy the food."

Martha rushed back to the market place. Mary brought the broom into the living room. Mary thought, "Martha mopped the floor yesterday; it doesn't need sweeping. After Jesus left last time, I thought of so many questions that I wished I'd asked him."

Mary propped the broom against a chair, found a pen and paper, and started making notes of questions to ask Jesus. She forgot about the cooking fire. Mary was still making notes when she heard a commotion outside. Martha opened the door and said, "Come on in and make yourselves at home!" Martha projected a silent scream toward Mary, "The broom, get the broom out of the living room!"

Mary jumped up, rushed to Jesus and said, "Oh, Jesus. Welcome! Come in. Have a seat. I have so many questions to ask you." Jesus sat in a chair; Mary sat on the floor, facing him.

Martha tried to hide the broom as she took it into the kitchen. Martha returned and asked Jesus and his disciples, "Can I get you something to drink? Well, make yourselves at home while Mary and I fix something to eat."
Mary didn't catch the hint. She continued sitting on the floor smiling up at Jesus. Martha thought, "Mary is never going to grow up and become a lady!"

Mary asked Jesus questions. Jesus answered each question with a story. Mary and the disciples enjoyed themselves.

From the kitchen came sounds of wood knocking against wood, pots banging against other pots and cabinet doors slamming.
Martha stormed into the room and interrupted Jesus' storytelling. Martha said, "Lord, don't you care. My sister is leaving all the serving to me. Please! Tell her to get up off the floor, get into the kitchen, and help me!"
Jesus answered, "Martha, Martha, you worry and fuss about so many things. However, few things are needed; only one thing is necessary. Mary made the right choice, and that one thing can't be taken from her."

Example # 3: **JUST A DONKEY** (Luke 19:28-38 Embellished)

Jack was a young colt donkey. Jack followed when his mother or daddy carried supplies to different farmers' markets. If a market was a long ways off, Jack's daddy gave their owner a ride and Jack's mother carried vegetables to the market. Jack dreamed of the day when he would be big enough to carry loads of vegetables or to give someone a ride. One Sunday morning, Jack's mother carried a load of vegetables to a village close to Jerusalem. Jack followed his mother. Jack liked to wander off and play, so Jack's owner put a halter on Jack and tied him to a post close to his mother. Then Jack's owner sat on a nearby porch to visit with other men.

Jack observed two men approaching. One man began to untie him. Jack brayed. His owner looked up and asked, "Why are you untying the donkey?"

One man responded to Jack's owner, "The master wants to borrow your colt donkey. He'll send him back."

The men untied the rope that restrained Jack to the post. They started to pull Jack away from his mother. Jack brayed, "Mamma! I want my mamma!"

Jack's mother said, "Jack, calm down. This is the day you've dreamed about. Today you get to work like your mother and daddy."

One man pulled on Jack's halter. The other walked behind punching Jack with a stick. Jack brayed all the way to the top of the hill, "Mamma! I want my mamma!" The two men complained, "I wish this stupid donkey would shut up!"

The men finally got Jack to the top of the hill. Men removed their coats and made a saddle for a man to ride Jack. One man sat on Jack. Another man started leading Jack down the hill toward the city of Jerusalem. People threw their coats and palm branches on the road. Crowds cheered and screamed, "Hosanna! Hosanna! Hosanna! Blessed is he who comes in the name of the Lord."

That night, Jack returned to the stable and described the excitement of his triumphant entrance into Jerusalem, "People cheered me. They shouted 'Hosanna.' They placed coats on the road for me to walk over. They put palm branches to soften the road for me, and they waved palm branches. Did I mention how they cheered?"

All week long Jack reminisced about crowds cheering and throwing coats and palm branches over the road as he made his triumphant entrance into Jerusalem.

The following Sunday, Jack slipped out of the stable. He made his way back up to the top of the hill and started marching down the hill into the city of Jerusalem.

Jack returned home with tears in his eyes. He cried to his mother, "Today, nobody cheered me. Some people were mean and hit me with sticks and shouted, 'Get out of the way, you stupid donkey!' Some people insulted me. They added a word to my name that's not a nice word. What happened mamma?"

Jack's mother replied, "Son, without Jesus, you're just a donkey."

I've heard storytellers tell biblical embellished stories. I've observed listeners' enthusiasm and heard their excitement as they talked about the embellished story. I recognize that many listeners prefer an embellished story over the true biblical version of the story.

But, the factual Bible story is God's story. Holy Spirit power is present when God's story is told as it is recorded in the Bible. A simple story that is a portion of God's story is a powerful story.

My concern is threefold:
1st Storytellers may never learn to tell accurate Bible stories because their listeners prefer embellished stories.
2nd Embellished Bible stories may misinform listeners.
3rd Listeners who are unfamiliar with the Bible story may receive a contaminated version of the Bible, because they think that the embellished story is the true story.

My suggestion is to consider embellished Bible stories as desserts to be served only to listeners who have recently read or heard the story as recorded in the Bible.

STORY-CASSEROLE SERMON
Circle One Theme With Several Stories

The term casserole refers to both a baking dish and the ingredients it contains. Casserole cookery is convenient because the ingredients are cooked and served in the same dish. A "casserole dish" usually refers to a deep, round or rectangular oven-proof container with a tight-fitting lid. It can be glass, metal, ceramic, or any other heat-proof material.

The casserole's ingredients usually consist of pieces of meat (such as chicken) or fish (such as tuna), various chopped vegetables, a starchy binder (such as flour), potatoes or pasta, and anything else the cook desires. Often, a crunchy topping such as cheese or breadcrumbs is added for texture and flavor. Liquids are released from the meat and vegetables during cooking. More liquid in the form of sauce, wine, beer, cider or vegetable juice may be added when the dish is being assembled. Casseroles are cooked slowly in the oven, often uncovered. Casseroles are often served as a one-dish meal and may be served in the vessel in which they were cooked.

The idea of casserole cooking as a one-dish meal became popular in America in the 1950's when new forms of lightweight metal and glassware appeared on the market.

Jesus never spoke to the crowds without telling parables (Mark 4:33-34). A parable is not a true story, but it communicates a truth. A parable is a fictitious, concise story that illustrates how a person should behave or what they should believe. It has a moral or religious life-lesson and illustrates a divine truth. A parable is a fictitious story about ordinary men and women, in familiar settings of life, whose everyday experiences teach a divine truth. Jesus always told stories whenever he preached. Sometimes Jesus explained his stories. Other times he told stories without giving any explanation.

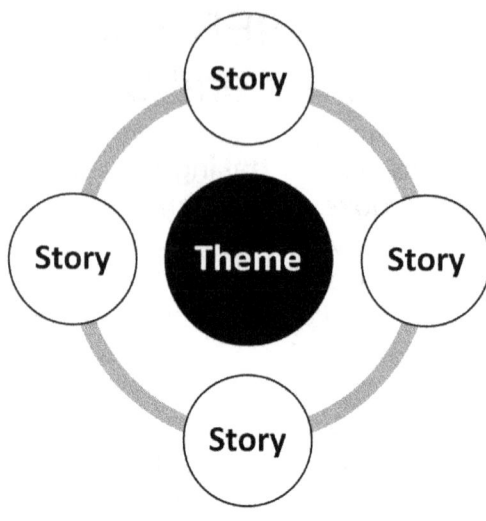

Often, when Jesus wanted to drive home a specific theme, he circled the theme with stories. He mentioned the theme, told a story, repeated the theme, told another story, and continued doing the same thing.

A Story-Casserole Sermon contains a mixture of stories that blend into one theme. The one theme is circled by several stories that illustrate it. Each time a story is told, the theme is mentioned. It would be like placing the theme idea in a hub of a wheel and circling the hub with several stories that relate to it.

The Story-Casserole Sermon imitates the way Jesus often preached. He took a theme idea and circled it with stories that illustrated the theme. He repeated the theme idea after each story or included the theme as a part of his stories. In Matthew 13, Jesus spoke about the Kingdom of Heaven. Jesus told eight stories to illustrate some aspects of the Kingdom of Heaven; seven times he said, "The Kingdom of Heaven is like."

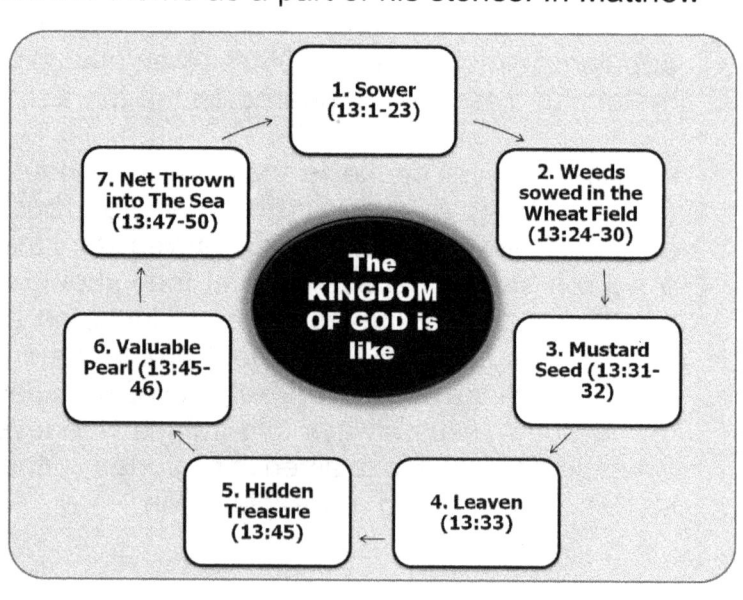

Preaching with Storytelling © Jackson Day

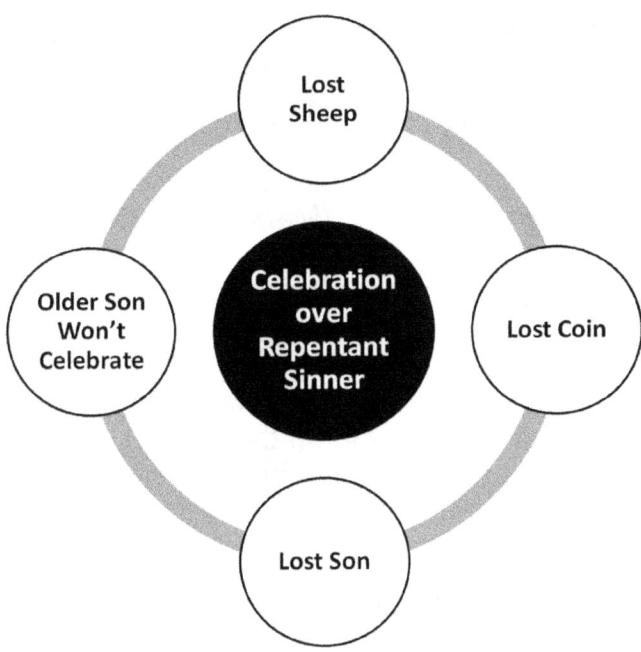

In Luke 15, Jesus circled the theme idea, "There will be rejoicing over the repentance of one sinner" with four stories: Lost Sheep, Lost Coin, Lost Younger Son and the Older Son Won't Celebrate.

Little exposition is given during the Story-Casserole Sermon. Little explanation is given to explain the theme, but several stories are told that illustrate it. The theme is repeated several times, usually before or after the telling of each story.

Selected stories may be Bible stories or they may be stories not found in the Bible. Each time a story is told, the theme is repeated.

The preacher, who imitates the way Jesus preached, needs to tell a mixture of stories that blend into one theme. The one theme is circled by several stories that illustrate it. Each time a story is told, the theme is mentioned. It would be like placing the theme idea in a hub of a wheel and circling the hub with several stories that relate to it.

EXAMPLE # 1: Story-Casserole Sermon

PRAYER IS FORGIVENESS
Mark 11:20-25

Jesus spoke about faith and prayer in Mark 11:20-25. Jesus said, "Have faith in God. I speak the truth, if anyone says to this mountain, 'Go, throw yourself into the ocean,' with no doubt in his heart but believing that what he says will happen, it'll be done for him. I tell you; therefore, everything you ask for in prayer, believe that you have it already, and it'll be yours. Prayer is not just asking; when you stand praying, if you hold anything against anyone who has wronged you, forgive him. Only then will your Father in heaven forgive you your sins" (Mark 11:20-25).

Jesus' disciples were good old boys from Galilee and would have known that the word "mountain" was often used as a slang word for a gigantic problem. One Sunday, I asked a high school football coach, "How did the football game go last Friday?"

Coach answered, "The wheel came off the cart."

I knew what Coach was talking about, but my wife is a city woman from Los Angeles. She thought Coach meant that a wheel came off the school bus taking the players to the game.

Jesus' disciples were good old boys from Galilee, and they knew that removing mountains usually referred to removing big problems. Sometimes we use the expression, "Making a mountain out of a mole hill." One thing is for sure, a wrong that is unforgiven develops into a gigantic mountain of a problem.

Theme:

Jesus taught: prayer is not just asking; when you stand praying, if you hold anything against anyone who has done you wrong, forgive him; only then will your Father in heaven forgive you of your sins.

Only the person who has been wronged has a need to forgive.

1. Heart Like a Computer File at Police Headquarters

Many people's hearts are similar to the computer program at a police headquarters. The police station has a computer program with files on wanted individuals and their criminal actions. You can ask, "What do you have on John Smith?" "What you got on Joe Blow?" The policeman can open the file and give you a printout of the wrongdoings of each of those people. The policeman can use the information to arrest the criminal and make him pay for his crimes.

We are often like that. We keep files in our minds of the wrongs others have done against us, people who we want to make them pay for their wrong. At anytime we can recall and share the information. Sometimes, with real grace, we leave the file closed and do not talk about the cases; yet, when necessary, the file is still there so that the cases can be brought to light and we can make them pay for the wrong they did against us.

As long as I have a police file against someone in my heart, I can't forgive them. With this computer file in my heart, I'm holding a grudge against the person who has wronged me. Obeying God's will becomes possible only after, by God's grace, I release the grudge against the person and allow God to delete the file. I must be as firm as a rock in this matter: I will not be a police computer with files stored in my heart that keep a file of the wrongs other people have done against me and my determination to make them pay for the wrongs.

Theme:
Jesus taught: prayer is not just asking; when you stand praying, if you hold anything against anyone who has done you wrong, forgive him; only then will your Father in heaven forgive you of your sins.

2. Parents Forgive Killer of their Children

On Monday morning, October 2, 2006, Charles Roberts carried an automatic rifle and four hundred rounds of ammunition into a one-room Amish school in Nickel Mines, Pennsylvania. Roberts ordered the boys and the teacher to leave. He tied the legs of the ten remaining girls. Roberts prepared to shoot them execution style. The oldest hostage, a thirteen-year old, begged Roberts, "Shoot me first and let the little ones go." He told the children, "I'm angry at God for taking my little daughter." Then he opened fire on all of them, killing five and leaving the others critically wounded. He shot himself as police stormed the building.

Blood was barely dry on the schoolhouse floor when Amish parents brought words of forgiveness to Roberts' family, the family of the man who had murdered their children. Fresh from the funerals where they had buried their own children, grieving Amish families accounted for half of the seventy-five people who attended the killer's burial. Roberts' widow was deeply moved as Amish families greeted her and her three children. The forgiveness went beyond talk and graveside presence – the Amish contributed money to a fund for the shooter's family.

Theme:
Jesus taught: prayer is not just asking; when you stand praying, if you hold anything against anyone who has done you wrong, forgive him; only then will your Father in heaven forgive you of your sins.

3. A Musician Forgives His Father

A musician who is not well-known has played instruments in some famous bands, and has sung backup for several well-known musicians.

The musician's father wanted him to be a banker. The first semester the aspiring musician went to the university, he signed up for some music courses. His father learned his son was taking music courses and sent him a letter saying, "I discovered you are studying music against my wishes. I notified the bank that you can no longer draw checks on my account. Neither can you come home, nor your brothers and sisters be allowed to write or call you."

The aspiring musician got a job as a waiter and stayed in school.

The next time the music student saw his father was three years later. The student was leaving a football game when he saw his father in the crowd. The son hollered, "Daddy, Daddy!" He made his way to his father and asked, "What are you doing here?"

His father answered, "I came to see a football game."

The son asked, "Were you going to look me up?"

The father answered, "I didn't come to see you; I came to see a football game!"

The young man graduated from the university and made a career playing in different bands and singing backup for some outstanding musicians.

The musician was thirty-six years old the next time he saw his father. His father was dying of cancer and the musician's brothers and sisters insisted that the father allow the musician son to visit him. The musician son returned home, only to hear his father angrily accuse him of being a rebellious son. But, with the other children insisting, the father agreed that all of his children could take his ashes to the lake where he loved to fish and scatter them.

A few weeks later, the father died. The musician joined his siblings in climbing into a boat and casting his father's ashes. The musician son made a choice: when he cast his father's ashes, he chose to also cast out the anger and resentment he felt toward his father.

Theme:
Jesus taught: prayer is not just asking; when you stand praying, if you hold anything against anyone who has done you wrong, forgive him; only then will your Father in heaven forgive you of your sins.

4. Unforgiving Sister at a Funeral

I went to the funeral of a long time friend. I knew this lady and her husband when we were in college together and they started dating. Years later, my wife and I worked together with the lady and her husband.

My wife and I were invited to join the family for a meal before the funeral service. The house was full, some eating in the kitchen, others in the dining room and others sitting on couches in the living room. Doris and I were sitting on a couch eating and talking to the sister of the deceased, who was sitting in a chair across from us.

The husband of the deceased entered the room and asked the sister, "Have you seen your brother?"

The sister answered, "Yes, I saw him."

The husband asked, "Did you speak to him?"

The sister answered, "No, I did not speak to him!"

The husband cried out, "There is no hope."

The sister said, "Everything is going to be all right."

The husband said, "It is not all right. My wife prayed all these years that you would start talking to your brother again. If you refuse to talk to him at your sister's funeral, there is no hope!"

The sister answered, "You don't know the whole story."

The husband of the deceased said, "No, I don't know the story. You've never told anyone why you refuse to talk to your brother."

The sister put her food on the coffee table, got up, walked out of the house, got in her car, and drove away. She left before her sister's funeral.

Theme:

Jesus taught: prayer is not just asking; when you stand praying, if you hold anything against anyone who has done you wrong, forgive him; only then will your Father in heaven forgive you of your sins.

5. Tim McGraw Forgives His Father

Reader's Digest had a story about country singer Tim McGraw. As a child, Tim McGraw had an abusive stepfather. Then the stepfather split. Afterwards, Tim's mother sometimes held three jobs at the same time. Sometimes she was on welfare. Once, they lived in a barn with hay on the floor.

Tim was eleven years old when he discovered his birth certificate and was astonished to read that his biological father was Tug McGraw, a famous baseball pitcher. The baseball star agreed to see Tim once. Then Tug refused to answer the boy's letters and calls.

Tim finished high school at eighteen. His father agreed to pay his university tuition, but made it clear that he wanted nothing else to do with his biological son. Tim graduated from the university and became a successful musician.

Tug, Tim's biological father and the former baseball hero, was fifty-eight years old when he found himself penniless, homeless, and dying with brain cancer. Tim brought to his home in Tennessee his biological father. His father had sex with a woman and as a result fathered Tim, but he wanted nothing else to do with his son. For five days, Tim sat by Tug's side and held his father's hand for up to twelve hours a day, even though Tug was often unconscious.

Two weeks after Tug died, Tim went into a music studio to record "Live Like You Were Dying."

Theme:
Jesus taught: prayer is not just asking; when you stand praying, if you hold anything against anyone who has done you wrong, forgive him; only then will your Father in heaven forgive you of your sins.

6. Unforgiving Parents

A young man went home to tell his parents that he was a homosexual. After the son's confession, the father went to his bedroom, returned with a pistol, removed five bullets, and placed the gun on the table with one bullet in the chamber. Then the father said, "Your mother and I are leaving the room and you can do the honorable thing that will save our family from shame."

The young man got up and left his parents' home, never to see them again.

The son was going against this parents' biblical and moral teachings. However, the parents were sinning against Jesus' teaching.

Theme:
Jesus taught: prayer is not just asking; when you stand praying, if you hold anything against anyone who has done you wrong, forgive him; only then will your Father in heaven forgive you of your sins.

7. Joseph Forgives his Brothers (Genesis 37-50)

The eleventh son born to Jacob was Joseph. Joseph was his father's favorite son. This provoked his brothers to hate him. When Joseph was seventeen years old, he dreamed that his brothers would bow down before him. He excitedly told his brothers about his dreams. His brothers became jealous and eventually sold him into slavery while leading their father to believe his favorite son had been killed by a wild animal.

Joseph was bought by Potiphar, who eventually recognized that the Lord was with Joseph. Potiphar made slave Joseph his administrator. Eventually, Potiphar's wife wrongly accused Joseph of trying to rape her. Joseph ended up in prison. The prison warden liked Joseph and he became a trustee responsible for the other prisoners. Through time, God elevated Joseph to become governor of Egypt.

During a severe drought, Joseph's brothers went to Egypt to buy food. Joseph was the man who sold food to foreigners. The brothers did not suspect that the man they stood before was their own brother. Joseph revealed himself to them and they were shocked to know he was alive. They feared that he would seek retribution. The family was reunited and lived together in Egypt. When their father passed away, the brothers feared that Joseph would finally show his hatred towards them (Genesis 50:15).

Joseph told his brothers, "Don't be afraid. I'm not in the place of God! You intended evil against me; God meant it for good, to bring to pass what is happening today, the saving of many lives. Don't be afraid; I'll provide for you and your little ones" (Genesis 50:19-21).

Theme:
Jesus taught: prayer is not just asking; when you stand praying, if you hold anything against anyone who has done you wrong, forgive him; only then will your Father in heaven forgive you of your sins.

8. Parable: Prodigal Son

Jesus told a parable, "A man had two sons. The younger son said to his father, `Father, give me my share of the estate.' The father divided property between his two sons. The younger son got together all his possessions and set off for a distant country where he wasted his wealth in wild living. After he had spent everything, a bad famine spread throughout that country, and the son was in great need. He found a job with a citizen of that country, who sent him to his fields to feed pigs. The son was so hungry he wanted to eat the bean pods that the pigs were eating, but no one gave him anything.

"The son came to his senses, and said to himself, `My father's hired men have food to spare, and here I am starving to death! I'll return to my father and tell him, 'Father, I've sinned against heaven; I've sinned against you. I don't deserve to be called your son; take me on as one of your hired men.' He got up and returned to his father.

"The son was still a long way off when his father saw him. The father was filled with compassion for him. The father ran to his son, embraced him and kissed him.

"The son said to him, `Father, I've sinned against heaven; I've sinned against you. I don't deserve to be called your son.'

"But the father called to his servants, `Hurry! Bring the best robe and put it on him. Put a ring on his finger and sandals on his feet. Bring the fattened calf and kill it. Let's celebrate with a feast. My son was dead and is now alive; he was lost and is now found.' They began to celebrate" (Luke 15:11-24).

Theme:

Jesus taught: prayer is not just asking; when you stand praying, if you hold anything against anyone who has done you wrong, forgive him; only then will your Father in heaven forgive you of your sins.

9. Older Son Refuses to Celebrate Return of His Brother

Now, I'm going to finish the previous parable told by Jesus.

"Meanwhile, the older son was in the field. He returned to the house and heard music and dancing. He called one of the servants and asked what was going on. The servant told him, `Your brother returned. Your father killed the fattened calf because your brother returned home safe and sound.'

"The older brother was so angry he refused to go into the house. His father went out and pleaded with him. The son answered his father, `Look! All these years I've been your slave. I never disobeyed your orders. Yet you never gave me even a young goat so I could celebrate with my friends. But, when this son of yours who wasted your property with wild living and prostitutes comes home, you kill the fattened calf for him!'

"The father replied, `Son, you're always with me. Everything I have is yours. But, we had to celebrate because your brother was dead and is alive again; he was lost and is found'" (Luke 15:25-31).

The elder brother remained outside the celebration.

Theme:
Jesus taught: prayer is not just asking; when you stand praying, if you hold anything against anyone who has done you wrong, forgive him; only then will your Father in heaven forgive you of your sins.

10. Crucifixion

Jesus was taken to the place called the Skull and was crucified, along with two criminals; one on his right, the other on his left. Jesus prayed, "Father, forgive them, for they don't know what they're doing" (Luke 23:33-34).

Theme:
Jesus taught: prayer is not just asking; when you stand praying, if you hold anything against anyone who has done you wrong, forgive him; only then will your Father in heaven forgive you of your sins.

11. Stoning of Stephen

Stephen was the first Christian martyr. Stephen spoke about Jesus with great wisdom. The enemies of Jesus' followers seized Stephen and took him to the Jewish Supreme Counsel. Stephen presented his argument to the Jewish Supreme Counsel and his listeners covered their ears, yelled at the top of their voices, rushed at him, dragged him out of the city and began to stone him.
While they were stoning him, Stephen prayed, "Lord Jesus, receive my spirit." Then Stephen fell on his knees and cried out, "Lord, don't hold this sin against them." Then Stephen died (Acts 7:54-60).

Theme:
Jesus taught: prayer is not just asking; when you stand praying, if you hold anything against anyone who has done you

wrong, forgive him; only then will your Father in heaven forgive you of your sins.

12. Heavy Potatoes

A seminary trains people who are preparing for Christian ministry. A seminary professor once told each of his students to bring a large clear plastic bag to class. The professor brought a large sack of potatoes.

The professor told each student to take a potato for each person who had wronged them and the student had not forgiven. He told the students to write the name of the wrongdoer and the date the person had wronged them. He told them to put the potatoes in their plastic bag. Some bags were quite heavy. The professor told the students to carry their bag with them everywhere for one week, putting it beside their bed at night, on the car seat when driving, and next to their desk at work.

The hassle of lugging their sack of potatoes around made it clear what a weight they were carrying spiritually. They had to pay attention to the sack all the time so they would not forget and leave it in an embarrassing place. Over a period of time, the condition of the potatoes deteriorated to a nasty smelly slime.

The sack of potatoes is a great metaphor for the price we pay for holding grudges against people who have wronged us. Often, we think of forgiveness as a gift to the other person, but it is also a gift to ourselves!

Only the person who has been wronged has a need to forgive.

Theme:
Jesus taught: prayer is not just asking; when you stand praying, if you hold anything against anyone who has done you wrong, forgive him; only then will your Father in heaven forgive you of your sins.

CONCLUSION:

We have wronged God and we desire that he forgives us of our sins. Only the person who has been wronged has a need to forgive. We need to forgive others in the same way as we want God to forgive us. Our prayers should include intentional forgiveness of those who have wronged us.

<u>EXAMPLE # 2</u>: **Story-Casserole Sermon**

BATTLE AGAINST ONESELF

Once upon a time, in a faraway land, cruel giants lived in a great big forest. Brave knights lived in a castle within the forest and protected the people of the forest and travelers from the cruel giants.

A magician created silver shields for each of the brave knights. Each time a knight would do a good deed, his silver shield would shine brighter. Each time the knight was brave in battle, his silver shield would shine brighter. However, if a knight were lazy, or cowardly, or arrogant, or proud, his shield would become increasingly cloudy until the knight would be ashamed to bear it. On rare occasions, if a knight showed exceptional courage or devotion to duty, a shiny golden star would appear in the center of his shield.

One day the cruel giants gathered to attack the castle and drive the brave knights from the forest. The lord of the castle gathered his knights to attack the giants before they reached the castle.

Young Sir Roland was the youngest knight in the castle. He recently acquired his shield and had yet to go into battle. He dreamed of distinguishing himself in battle so his silver shield would shine brighter. But, the lord of the castle ordered young Sir Roland to stay behind and guard the castle's drawbridge. Young Sir Roland was to prevent anyone from crossing the drawbridge over the moat and entering the castle while the knights were on the battle field.

Young Sir Roland felt embarrassed as he stood at the gate while the knights rode their horses to the battle ground. However, he stood erect at the gate holding his new silver shield with his left hand and his spear with his right. He stood guard to prevent anyone from crossing the drawbridge over the moat to enter the castle while the other knights were distinguishing themselves in battle.

Eventually, a lone knight carrying a cloudy dull shield rode up wearily. The knight had a few scratches, but claimed he had been wounded in battle. The knight with the cloudy dull shield offered to trade places with young Sir Roland. He would stand guard at the drawbridge, out of harm's way, and let young Sir Roland seek glory on the battle ground. Young Sir Roland wanted to leap at the chance, but replied, "The lord of the castle ordered me to guard the drawbridge. I can't even allow you to cross the drawbridge and enter the castle."

At the noon hour, an old woman approached the castle and begged for bread and water. The old woman said she had been near the battle, and the knights were doing poorly. The old woman accused the young knight of being a coward who was afraid to join his companions on the battle ground. Young Sir Roland gave the old woman bread and water, but resisted the temptation to prove to her his bravery. He wanted to be on the battle ground, but had orders from the lord of the castle to stand guard at the drawbridge.

Next, an old man in a long cloak appeared across the moat and said, "I'm a magician; I want to help the knights protect the people of the forest. I'll give you a magic sword that you can use in the battle to save your comrades from destruction. Take the magic sword, leave the drawbridge, and join the battle in the forest."

Young Sir Roland felt so tempted to join the other knights on the battle ground that he moved back across the moat to raise the drawbridge to cut himself off from the strange old man. Suddenly, the magician threw off his cloak and began to grow into a great giant. He howled at young Sir Roland in frustration before turning back to the forest.

Eventually the company of knights rode back, battle weary, but victorious. They approached the gate and stopped in wonder. Shining on young Sir Roland's shield, was a shiny golden star. The knights did not understand how someone who had not fought in battle could earn the shiny, golden star. The lord of the castle explained that the hardest battles a knight must fight are against oneself and not against an armed enemy. Young Sir Roland had stood guard at the drawbridge when he wanted to be on the battle field. Young Sir Roland had fought the hardest battle of the day.

It is not just in a make-believe mythical land of fables that people must fight hard battles against themselves. The Bible gives many examples of people who fought battles against themselves. Most lost the battle.

Jesus warned his disciples, "Watch and pray so that you will not fall into temptation. The spirit is willing, but the body is weak" (Matthew 26:41 NIV).

Paul describes the battle each person must fight against himself in Galatians 5:17, "For the sinful nature desires what is contrary to the Spirit, and the Spirit what is contrary to the sinful nature. They are in conflict with each other, so that you do not do what you want" (Galatians 5:17 NIV).

Paul described a battle that goes on inside each Christian. God's Spirit lives within believers in Jesus, and he opposes evil and encourages believers to do things that please God. However, the sinful nature within each person desires to do things that are wrong.

Theme:
The hardest battles you must fight are oftentimes the ones you must fight against yourself.

1. Cain Lost the Battle Against His Anger (Genesis 4:1-8)

Adam and his wife Eve had two sons, Cain and Abel. Abel became a herdsman and kept flocks; Cain became a farmer and worked the soil. Cain fought and won the battle against the elements and the thorns, and he raised a crop.

Cain brought some produce from his farm as an offering to the Lord. But, Abel brought choice cuts of meat from the firstborn of his flock. The Lord accepted Abel and his offering, but rejected Cain and his offering.

Cain became very angry; his face was dark with rage. The Lord asked Cain, "Why are you angry? Why is your face so dark with rage? If you do what is right, I will accept you. But, if you don't do what is right, sin is crouching at your door waiting to pounce; it is out to get you, but you must tame it."

One day Cain said to his brother Abel, "Let's go out into the field." While they were in the field, Cain attacked his brother Abel and killed him.

A family took their dog camping with them in Montana. At night they tied their dog to a post outside their trailer. The dog kept barking, wanting inside the trailer. Another camper became so angry at the barking dog that he took an ax and shut the dog up permanently. The man then got a good night's sleep, but was later sentenced to four years in prison.

Anger is like a wild animal crouching at your door waiting to pounce; it is out to get you, but you must tame it.

Theme:
Some of the hardest battles you must fight are oftentimes the ones you must fight against your own anger. "Watch and pray so that you will not fall into temptation. The spirit is willing, but the body is weak" (Matthew 26:41 NIV).

2. Noah Lost the Battle Against Strong Drink
    (Genesis 9:20-24)

Noah fought the battle against the ridicule of his neighbors as he obeyed God and built an ark in a place where it had never rained. After the flood, Noah became a farmer and planted a vineyard. He made wine, drank it, got drunk, and passed out naked inside his tent (9:20-27).

A new Christian was tempted by co-workers into taking a few drinks. He went home drunk. His twelve-year old son was having some friends sleep over. The drunk father embarrassed his son.

The next day, the father asked his son's forgiveness. However, his son never again invited any friends to their home.

Losing the battle against alcohol, drugs, and pornography can result in addictions that control our minds and actions.

Theme:
Some of the hardest battles you must fight are oftentimes the ones you must fight against things that can dominate you and turn you into an addict. "Watch and pray so that you will not fall into temptation. The spirit is willing, but the body is weak" (Matthew 26:41 NIV).

3. Abram Lost the Battle Against Imaginary Fears
(Genesis 12:10-13)

A severe famine came to Canaan, and Abram went down to Egypt. Just before they entered Egypt, he told his wife Sarai, "You are very beautiful. When the Egyptians see you, they'll kill me but will let you live. Therefore, tell them you are my sister, so that my life will be spared" (Genesis 12:10-13).

A daughter lived in a distant city from her parents. She received the message that her parents were hospitalized after a car wreck. Before she reached the airport to fly to her parents' home, the daughter began planning for her parents' funeral. While flying home, she became convinced that her sister and sister-in-law would go to her parents' home and get all her mother's jewelry. The daughter arrived at the airport, rented a car, drove to her parent's home and selected the choice pieces of her mother's jewelry. Then she drove to the hospital, only to discover that her parents had only suffered some broken bones.

The origin of imaginary fears is in the mind of the person with the fear. Some children have imaginary fears of monsters hiding under the bed. Some adults have phobias that co-workers are always talking about them, or their spouse is unfaithful. During the present-day financial crisis, many people are battling imaginary fears. They imagine they'll lose their job; then the bank will repossess their car and foreclose on their house; then their spouse will leave them and take the children; then they will never see the children again.

Theme:
Some of the hardest battles you must fight are oftentimes the ones you must fight against imaginary fears. "Watch and pray so that you will not fall into temptation. The spirit is willing, but the body is weak" (Matthew 26:41 NIV).

4. David Lost the Battle Against Lust (2 Samuel 11:1-27)

The boy David fought giant Goliath and won. Years later, David became king of Israel and he won every military battle he fought.

One day, David ate his lunch and took a siesta. He got up from his bed and walked around on the flat roof of his palace. From the vantage point of the roof, David saw his neighbor's wife, Bathsheba, a beautiful woman, bathing. David sent messengers to get her. She came to him, and he went to bed with her. David won the battle against a giant, but lost the battle against his lust for a little woman.

Many have lost the battle against lust. The yet-to-marry feel that the sex act would be the ultimate thrill, and we who are married have the feelings that relations with someone other than our spouse would be more exciting.

Theme:
Some of the hardest battles you must fight are oftentimes the ones you must fight against your own lust. "Watch and pray so that you will not fall into temptation. The spirit is willing, but the body is weak" (Matthew 26:41 NIV).

5. Rehoboam Lost the Battle Against Greed
(1 Kings 12:1-16)

King Solomon was the wealthiest king in the world. The Israelites resented the high taxes and forced labor that contributed to Solomon's wealth. Solomon died and his son Rehoboam became the wealthiest king in the world. Israel's leaders told him, "Your father put a heavy tax yoke on us and burdened us with hard work. Loosen up the harsh labor burden and the heavy tax yoke he put on us, and we'll serve you."

Rehoboam replied, "My father made your yoke heavy; I'll make it even heavier. My father beat you with whips; I'll beat you with chains!" The vast majority of the Israelites rebelled against Rehoboam and he lost most of his kingdom.

Rehoboam had inherited the wealthiest kingdom in the world; however, his greed demanded more from his people, and he lost his kingdom.

Black spider monkeys look like gigantic spiders when they are suspended by their tails. There is a market for healthy uninjured spider monkeys. Trappers in South America's rain forest want to trap spider monkeys without injuring them. A trapper puts hazelnuts into a large jar with a top just big enough for a spider monkey to slip a relaxed hand into it. The jar is glued to a post. The monkey slips his hand into the narrow opening of the jar and grabs a handful of hazelnuts. But his closed hand around the nuts is too big to pull out of the jar. The monkey could open his hand, release the nuts, and pull his hand out of the jar; but he won't let go of the nuts. The monkey stays stuck, chattering and screaming. The trapper picks the monkey up at his leisure and puts him into a cage. The monkey is trapped because he refuses to let go of the nuts.

The person, who is never grateful for what he has and who is always grasping for more, finds himself caught in a monkey-trap of greed.

Theme:
Some of the hardest battles you must fight are oftentimes the ones you must fight against your own greed. "Watch and pray so that you will not fall into temptation. The spirit is willing, but the body is weak" (Matthew 26:41 NIV).

6. Peter Lost the Battle Against Fear of Pending Danger
(John 18:15-18, 25-27)

Jesus had been arrested and was taken to the high priest's house. Peter followed Jesus into the high priest's courtyard.

The girl at the gate asked Peter, "Aren't you one of that man's disciples?"

Peter replied, "No, I'm not." A rooster crowed.

Peter sat with the guards and warmed himself at the fire.

The servant girl said to those standing around, "This fellow was with Jesus from Nazareth!"

Peter denied it, "That's not true!"

Those standing near said to Peter, "Surely you are one of them, because you talk like them."

Peter called down curses on himself and swore, "I don't know this cursed man you're talking about."

Just then, a rooster crowed the second time. Peter remembered Jesus' words, "Before the rooster crows twice you will deny that you know me three times." Peter started crying.

In the 1950's, I rode to school inside a big yellow bus. We passed black children riding to another school on the back of a farmer's flat bed truck. In the 1950's, the person in Alabama who declared that segregation was unjust would have put himself and his family in danger.

Sometimes it's dangerous to tell the truth or stand for right when you are surrounded by people who disagree with you.

Theme:
Some of the hardest battles you must fight are oftentimes the ones you must fight when it is dangerous to tell the truth or do what is right. "Watch and pray so that you will not fall into temptation. The spirit is willing, but the body is weak" (Matthew 26:41 NIV).

7. Peter Lost the Battle Against Peer Pressure
(Galatians 2:11-16)

Paul and Barnabas were helping the non-Jewish church in the city of Antioch. Peter, a Jew, visited the non-Jewish church. He sat at the table and ate with non-Jews. However, Jewish Christians from Jerusalem arrived in Antioch, and they refused to eat at the same table with non-Jews. Peter separated himself from the non-Jews to eat with the Jews from Jerusalem. Other Jewish Christians followed Peter's example.

My wife and I were guests in the home of a policewoman who came home distressed. She had seen her pastor's son in jail. The previous night, her pastor's son slipped out the window of his house to drink beer with some popular classmates. He agreed to drive them to a store. The classmates went inside and robbed the store. The store owner grabbed a gun and the young robbers shot him. The classmates ran out of the store and the pastor's son drove the car away. The pastor's son was arrested as the driver of the getaway car, and an accomplice to murder committed during an armed robbery. That night of giving in to peer pressure ruined his life.

Peer pressure is the influence from family, friends, classmates, coworkers, or neighbors to behave in a manner similar or acceptable to them. Bad peer pressure coerces you into doing something that everyone else is doing, but you know it's wrong.

Theme:
Some of the hardest battles you must fight are oftentimes the ones you must fight against peer pressure. "Watch and pray so that you will not fall into temptation. The spirit is willing, but the body is weak" (Matthew 26:41 NIV).

8. Jesus Won the Battle Against Wanting to Get His Way Instead of Doing God's Will (Matthew 26:36-44)

The night before Jesus was arrested, he went to the Garden of Gethsemane. Jesus fell with his face to the ground and prayed, "My Father, if it's possible, may this cup be taken from me. Yet not as I will, but as you will."

He prayed a second time, "My Father, if it's not possible for this cup to be taken away unless I drink it, may your will be done."

He prayed a third time, saying the same thing. Jesus wanted to flee the crucifixion, but he remained in the Garden, allowing the soldiers to arrest him.

The author of Hebrews tells us, "Because he (Jesus) himself suffered when he was tempted, he is able to help those who are being tempted" (Hebrew 2:18 NIV).

Jesus was tempted and won the battle against wanting to get his way instead of doing the Father's will. Jesus won the battle against himself. Therefore, Jesus is able to help us when we fight the battle against ourselves.

CONCLUSION
1. If you have lost the battle against yourself and have yielded to temptation, confess your sin to God and ask his forgiveness.
2. Be aware of the battles you have lost against yourself in the past. Lost battles show your weakness, and where you risk losing another battle in the future. Be on guard.
3. Give thanks to God that He stands ready to forgive us and give us new opportunities when we lose a battle against ourselves.
4. If you are presently fighting a hard battle against yourself, and you want us to pray that you will depend on Jesus to help you win your battle against yourself, raise your hand as a sign that you are requesting our prayers.

Some of the hardest battles you must fight are oftentimes the ones you must fight against yourself: anger, substance that can control your mind, imaginary fears, lust, greed, pending danger, peer pressure, and doing what you want instead of doing what God wants you to do.

"Watch and pray so that you will not fall into temptation. The spirit is willing, but the body is weak." (Matthew 26:41 NIV).

"Because he (Jesus) himself suffered when he was tempted, he is able to help those who are being tempted" (Heb 2:18 NIV).

ONE-DISH MEAL
One-Story Sermon

The one-dish meal can easily pack the whole food pyramid into one convenient skillet, pot, crockpot or casserole dish. My wife often makes a one-dish stew in the crockpot or prepares a chicken pot pie for just the two of us. The whole meal–vegetables and meat–comes to the table in a single pot, bowl, or dish. The one-dish meal has no additional side dishes such as green beans, rice, or other accompaniments. The one-dish meal is a balanced meal; that means, no separate all-vegetable or all-meat dishes.

The preacher can do a One-Story Sermon. The one-story is the sermon itself. The sermon consists of reading the Scripture text and telling one-story with no explanation given. Sometimes the reading of the Scripture is before the story; sometimes it is included in the story; sometimes it comes after telling the story.

The Christian community has always experienced preachers who taught through storytelling instead of interpreting the scriptures. They communicated biblical principles in everyday stories, similar to what Jesus did in telling parables. Jesus told parables to put his listeners on the road to truth. Jesus' parable-stories didn't illustrate his message; parable-stories were his message. The preacher can imitate Jesus by crafting stories that put listeners on the road to truth.

The story chosen for the One-Story sermon deals with people facing common life-issues, but its overtone reaches into biblical life-lessons. The story has a subtext that suggests a biblical lesson about how people should behave or what they should believe. The subtext biblical lesson may be unspoken, but it is obvious to observant listeners. The story makes a point that observant listeners should understand. All listeners hear a good story, while spiritually observant listeners hear a word from God.

The preacher of the One-Story Sermon treats his listeners similar to the way an artist treats those who observe his work of art. At the end of a novel, theater, movie, or play, the author does not come forward and tell the audience what his work of art meant. The work of art is open-ended. The open-endedness allows the audience to participate in the completion of the work of art in their own lives. In the same way, after the One-Story, the preacher does not tell his listeners what his story meant, nor the ideas they should find in the story. The open-endedness of the One-Story Sermon allows the listeners, guided by the Holy Spirit, to participate in the completion of the sermon in their own lives.

In the One-Story Sermon, the preacher is not in control of the interpretation of the text for the congregation. The preacher must have confidence in both the Holy Spirit and his listeners. He trusts the Holy Spirit to guide listeners to see truth through his story. He trusts the story to speak to listeners in a more relevant way than if he explains ideas.

The One-Story Sermon imitates the way Jesus usually used parables. Jesus spoke to the crowds in parables. In fact, he only spoke to them in parables (Matthew 13:34). When Jesus spoke to the crowds, he only told stories. His message was the stories he told. Most of the time when Jesus told a parable, he did not explain the parable to his listeners. Jesus often finished a parable with the words, "He who has ears, let him hear" (Matthew 13:43). Peter once asked Jesus to explain a parable and Jesus answered, "Are you so dull?" (Matthew 15:16). Jesus told his parables and expected his listeners to figure things out for themselves.

EXAMPLE: **One-story Sermon**

TAKING PAVEMENT TO HEAVEN

A baby boy was born to Mr. and Mrs. Penton. His parents called him Robert Andrew Penton. However, everyone called him Bobby. His parents started taking Bobby to church when he was a baby in their arms. When Bobby became a young boy, sometimes his parents would stay home on Sundays, but even then they would drive Bobby to church and pick him up afterwards.

When Bobby was sixteen years old, his parents gave him a second-hand car, the car that his mother had been driving. His parents told him, "We've always insisted you go to church, but now we're going to leave the choice to you. You can continue if you wish, or you can stop going."

Bobby answered, "I believe in God, I believe the Bible to be the word of God, I believe God answers prayers, and I enjoy going to church. I'll continue going to church."

Bobby began to pray that God would help him make good grades in high school and he made the honor roll. Bobby prayed that God would help him obtain a scholarship to a prestigious university; an elite university offered Bobby an academic scholarship.

Bobby went to the university and introduced himself as Robert. Robert prayed that he would make good grades. Robert made the Dean's list. When he was in his sophomore year, Robert prayed that he would find a girlfriend who would make him a good wife. Robert fell in love with Laura, a beautiful, talented young lady who also loved the church. During his senior year, Robert prayed that he would find a job where he could afford to get married. He sent out resumes and went to job fairs. Robert was offered a good paying job for someone just out of college. He would start to work a month after graduation. Robert prayed that Laura would be willing to be his fiancee. Laura said, "Yes!" Robert and Laura became engaged.

The week after graduating from the university, Robert and Laura were married. Robert maxed out his credit cards paying for their honeymoon, first month's rent in a furnished apartment and food until his first paycheck. Robert prayed that he would be able to pay off his credit card debts within a year; he was able to pay them off in eleven months. Robert was still driving the car his parents gave him for his sixteenth birthday, and he prayed to be able to buy their first new car. He was able to buy and make payments on a new SUV. Then he prayed that he would get a job promotion so they could afford to buy a house. The promotion came and they bought their own home.

Then Robert prayed that God would give Laura and him children. First came a baby boy; two years later a baby girl was born.

Then Robert prayed for another promotion so they could afford a large home with yard space, where the children could play, and in a community with excellent schools. With the promotion, people at work started calling him Mr. Robert Penton. Mr. and Mrs. Robert Penton were able to buy a larger home in a more expensive neighborhood that had an outstanding school system. Each time Mr. Robert Penton prayed for a promotion, he was promoted. The president of the company retired and Mr. Penton prayed that the job would be his; Mr. Robert Penton became the company's president.

Mr. Robert Penton kept praying for his children: that they would be healthy, that they would do well in school, that they would get into elite universities, that they would make good choices when they married, and that his children would make Laura and him grandparents. Each of the things he prayed for happened.

Mr. Penton was fifty-nine years old when he was diagnosed with terminal lung cancer. The doctor said he probably had four months to live, six months at the most. Mr. Penton prayed, "God, I know they say you can't take it with you, but you've answered all my prayers. I want to be able to take my wealth with me. Now Lord, you know I got to be president of the company by working hard, being honest and putting in long hours. I did not step on people's backs to climb the ladder of success. I did my best for the company and I prayed for you to open the doors of opportunity. So, let me take my wealth with me to Heaven."

Mr. Robert Penton felt sure that God gave him an affirmative answer. Mr. Penton searched his Bible and he could not find any mention of stocks and bonds, nor dollars in Heaven. But he found several mentions of gold in Heaven. So Mr. Penton ordered his broker to convert his stocks and bonds to gold and sent it to his home. A full container of gold was shipped to Mr. Robert Penton's home.

Mr. Penton reached the pearly gates of heaven, and he met Saint Peter. Robert Penton was so excited when he looked beyond the pearly gates and saw the container with his gold. Simon Peter's brother Andrew was watching when Robert Penton excitedly opened his container of gold.

Later Andrew asked Peter, "Was Robert Penton able to bring his wealth to Heaven in that container?"

Peter answered, "Yes, that container contains all his wealth."

Andrew asked, "What was in it? Does it contain records of sick people he visited?"

Peter answered, "No."

Andrew asked, "Does it contain records of the hungry people he fed, the poor he helped, the needy he helped get jobs, the under-privileged children he tutored, the mistreated for whom he obtained justice?"

Peter answered, "No, no, no, no, no."

Andrew asked, "Does it contain the names of people who are coming here because he showed them the way?"

Peter answered, "No."

Andrew asked, "Well, what is in the container?"

Peter answered, "Pavement, nothing but pavement!"

Andrew said, "I thought Robert Penton was a man who knew how to pray."

Peter answered, "Oh yes, Robert Penton knew how to pray with faith, and God answered his prayers. However, his prayers were always about himself, his wife, his two children, those four and no more. His prayers of faith were sweet perfume reaching up to God. But God always waited for more from Robert's prayers. He wanted to see Robert Penton use his prayers to bring blessings on others."

Andrew asked, "Well, what are we going to do with all that gold? The main streets of heaven are already paved. The streets that pass in front of the mansions are paved, and so are the streets that pass in front of the cottages."

Peter answered, "I've already talked to the Lord about it. The Lord said we can pave the path that goes up to the travel trailer that will be Robert Penton's home in glory."

Read: Matthew 6:19-21, 33

Jesus said, "Do not store up for yourselves treasures on earth, where moth and rust destroy, and where thieves break in and steal. But store up for yourselves treasures in heaven, where moth and rust do not destroy, and where thieves do not break in and steal. For where your treasure is, there your heart will be also" (Mt 6:19-21 NIV).

Jesus also said, "But seek first his kingdom and his righteousness, and all these things will be given to you as well" (Mt 6:33 NIV).

CHEF'S CREATIONS
Communicate Truth Through Original Stories

Chef's Creations are dishes that a chef invents. The chef does not use a recipe from a book or from another chef. He does not imitate someone else's cooking. The dish is original with him.

The storyteller can craft original stories to communicate divine truths. The one who crafts stories in this manner is imitating Jesus who crafted stories, called parables, to communicate divine truths. Jesus never spoke without telling stories. The apostle Paul spoke and wrote using the philosophical discourse of the educated. The New Testament records both the stories of Jesus and the writing of philosophical Paul. Preachers should value both storytelling and the interpretative-philosophical emphasis. Preachers with ability to craft stories should use this ability to communicate divine truth. Preachers need to take a new look at Jesus' method of communicating his message. It is time for preachers to imitate Jesus and learn to speak in stories.

Often a story can express a truth that could not be expressed in any way but through a story; similar to the way music can express emotions that could never be portrayed through a speech. A story may simplify a complex teaching, allowing listeners to learn the complex concept via a short, simple story.

The preacher crafts a story with the desire to convey biblical teachings. The story becomes the vehicle with which to transport spiritual truth. The story becomes a forum to declare God's message. The story-crafter allows his perspectives to overflow into his stories. He crafts stories that hint at the teaching found in Scripture. He incarnates the truth into story. Artistic craftsmanship becomes a secondary concern to communicating truth through story.

Even if listeners are unwilling to hear the naked truth, the truth must still be told. Clothing the naked truth in story is a way to get truth out.

The deepest insights about life will not be found in theological philosophical statements, but in stories about everyday relationships, ordinary happenings, and commonplace lives.

The storytelling-preacher doesn't craft stories for children, but for listeners who are childlike, whether they are five, twenty-five, fifty, or seventy-five years old. The storyteller crafts or finds stories that have meaning for listeners who desire to grow in the realms of relationship with God and people, wisdom and love.

The original crafted story may be a short illustration or it can be a long story-sermon.

To help you prepare your original stories, I am including a summary of suggestions for crafting a story found in my book, *Story Crafting*.

The typical story adheres to the following three-part structure:

Beginning:
- The story begins with an initial-situation that establishes equilibrium, a stable situation where things make sense and key-characters are comfortable in their setting. The beginning establishes a baseline of normality. The initial-situation will introduce the key-character(s) who lives in a clearly described time and place.

- Next comes the initial-problem, an upset that challenges the equilibrium of the initial-situation. The initial-problem upsets the normality; it threatens the status quo and challenges the old order. The stable situation disappears with the initial-problem. The initial-problem is an inciting event that identifies a problem or need, and hints that trouble is on the way.

Middle:
- The <u>sequence of events</u> develops the core of the story with problem situations, progressive complications, conflicts, dialogues, outside interference, and aborted attempts at resolution.

Ending:
- The story ends with a <u>final-situation</u>. The <u>final-situation</u> brings a resolution. The <u>initial-problem</u> that caused the upset is resolved. A new normality, a new equilibrium is established. This new equilibrium is not like the old. The key-character(s) gain new strength and understanding from having their world shaken.

CRAFTING A STORY

The following guidelines will help beginner storytellers craft stories for telling.

1. Choose the key-character(s)

Characters are at the core of every story. Determine who are the key-character(s). In most stories, the key-characters will be people. However, key-characters may be non-humans, such as animals, plants or objects that are given people-like characteristics.

Organize the story around characters. Characters act, experience conflict and undergo struggles. If the storyteller doesn't create believable characters, listeners won't care what happens to them.

Wounded characters make for interesting stories. People desire to be rich, healthy, strong, and good looking, but such characters make for dull stories.

The more real the key-characters are to the storyteller, the more listeners will be drawn to hear the story. The storyteller must see his characters with clarity if he expects his listeners to see them at all.

Build characters through action and dialogues, not through description. Dialogue can include internal dialogue, where a character talks to himself. Also, describe characters' emotions through action.

Use nouns and verbs to make a character come alive. Don't say someone walks slowly when you can say he pokes, shuffles, lumbers, strolls, lolls or saunters.

Show; don't tell. Don't use abstract descriptions to describe a character; use concrete descriptions. Don't describe a character by saying, "She was beautiful." Instead, give details that will lead your listeners to conclude, "She was beautiful." *Example*: Say, "When she walked down the street, young men who passed her turned their heads and gazed at her."

2. Setup the initial-situation of the story

The initial-situation puts the key-character(s) into a situation that has a history and presents the back-story, the essential details about the key-character's past that story-listeners need to know. The initial-situation introduces the key-character who lives in a clearly described time and place. The initial-situation establishes equilibrium, a stable situation where things make sense and the key-character is comfortable in his setting. Establish the initial-situation by saying everything that needs to be said in as few words as possible.

Spell out the story-goal of the key-character(s). The initial-situation should introduce the story-goal of the key-character(s). The key-character's story-goals present the ambition, need, dream or object of desire that is of great importance to him.
The character's story-goal could be something concrete like buying a new car.
The story-goal could be an abstract goal such as having a second chance after betraying friends.
The story-goal could be a combination of the abstract and the concrete. *Example*: The office worker who feels worthless sitting behind a desk in a cubicle could see the acquisition of a motorboat as the key to regaining his self-respect.

Establish the initial-problem that upsets and challenges the equilibrium of the initial-situation. The initial-situation presents the story-goal of the key-character(s). Then, the initial-problem appears in the form of a person or circumstance which threatens to deny the key-character(s) his story-goal.

The initial-problem becomes the "big hook" that incites and captures the listeners' attention. It creates a hunger for the knowledge of how the key-character will obtain his story-goal.

The initial-problem gives the story-listeners a sense that something is imminent, that certain events are set in relentless motion and that bigger problems are on the way. It helps the listeners to see trouble is coming before the key-crisis actually arrives.

3. Organize the sequence of events

Remember, the initial-situation gives the setting for the story and the key-character's story-goal. The initial-problem shakes up the initial-situation and propels the key-character on a quest to reach his story-goal. Then follows a series of events as the story develops with its pattern of problems, dilemmas, conflicts, setbacks, and aborted attempts at reaching the story-goal until the story has a final result. Each event that complicates the initial-problem, or each attempt at finding a resolution, is an event within the story. Each subdivision, plot, plan, turn of events or new development is an event within the story.

The sequence of events would be the story-plan written in simple outline form. It is the road map that gives direction to the story. I suggest that the sequence of events first be written using one or two sentence statements to describe each event in the order they will be told. This is a tool for the storyteller and may be too cryptic for anyone but the storyteller to follow. After he is satisfied with his cryptic sequence of events, the storyteller may expand on each event from its one or two sentences to turn them into paragraphs.

Within the sequence of events, conflict adds spice to a story. Conflict is the soul of a story. The greater the conflict, the greater the attention of the listeners. The key-character has his story-goal. He must struggle against forces that block that desire. He must crash into cruel, uncooperative situations or people, and deal with opposing forces. A story worth listening to doesn't just portray the rosy side. It portrays the dark side of life and deals with antagonistic events. Conflict may be real or imaginary.

Determine where the key-crisis happens in the sequence of events. The key-crisis is the climax of the story and is usually built up from preceding conflicts. Determine where the key-crisis happens in the sequence of events.

4. Establish the final-situation of the story

The story continues until a conclusion is reached that establishes a final-situation. The final-situation brings a resolution. The initial-problem that caused the upset is resolved. A new normality, a new equilibrium is established. This new equilibrium is not like the old. The key-character(s) gains new strength and understanding from having his world shaken. The story ends with the final-situation.

REVISING THE CRAFTED STORY

After the storyteller has crafted the structure of his story, he needs to make revisions. He needs to give special attention to key-repetitions and key-attitudes. He needs to transform "telling" into "showing," and he needs to reduce the story to the essential facts.

1. Work on key-repetitions

Events in an oral story are often tied together by words, themes, patterns, facts or ideas that are repeated, either exactly or with minor variations. The oral storyteller should intentionally use repetition in order to emphasize, to build a climax, or to express strong emotions.

Repetitions in a story can take a variety of forms. Certain words, the same phrase, the same theme, similar actions, a song, a chant, the same gesture, certain patterns, facts or ideas can be repeated; either exactly or with minor variations. Repetitions help both the storyteller and listeners to remember.

Review the sequence of events to determine if repetitions have already been included or if more need to be inserted. Most storytellers need to weave repetitions into their story after establishing the sequence of events.

2. Consider key-attitudes to be expressed in the story

Stories express attitudes, feelings, values, and emotions. The storyteller needs to determine the attitudes he wishes to express in the story in order to help his listeners feel the desired emotions.

Within the story, describe actions to present the character's attitudes. Show; don't tell. Instead of saying the mother was concerned about her son, describe the mother sitting up until the son returned home.

Review the story's sequence of events and consider what attitude the storyteller desires to express with each event and with each character. Then make revisions or additions that include concrete descriptions, actions and dialogues which convey those attitudes. Avoid telling a fact if you can show emotion to the fact with dialogue, action or description. If you want to show that a character named Tom is angry, have Tom punch a hole in the sheetrock with his fist.

3. Transform "telling" into "showing"

Show; don't tell. Review your story to change where you told instead of showed. If you used abstract descriptions to describe a character or setting, transform it into concrete descriptions. If you said something similar to, "George was a poor, dirty child," transform it to, something like, "Little ten-year old George looked at his torn, ragged, unwashed, unpatched overalls. His mother had not told him to take a bath, so he had not bathed before going to school. Little George looked down at his dirty bare feet."

If you "described" a story-character's moral-character, revise your story to "show" his moral-character. Instead of saying, "Andrew was cruel," say, "After fighting with his girlfriend, Andrew ran his car off the side of the road in order to run over a dog that was following a little boy."

If you "described" an attitude, revise your story to "show" the attitude. Don't say, "Martha was sad," when you can say, "Martha woke up with her pillow wet with tears."

4. **Reduce the story to the essential facts**

When preparing the story, most storytellers include needless details that clutter the story and take unnecessary time to tell. Remember the principle: "Less is more," when revising the story. The less there is in the story, the more impact it has. Therefore, anything that can be cut should be cut. If narration can be removed and the story could still stand on its feet, then cut it. Eliminate all detail, dialogue, facts and events that aren't essential to move the story forward. The storyteller will probably need to eliminate 20% to 50% of the material he included in the first crafting of his story. Drastic surgery is needed to get crafted stories ready to tell. I usually take more time revising a story than I did in first crafting it.

<u>Example of Story I Crafted</u>: **BROTHER LIKE THAT**

Structure of the Crafted Story

KEY-ELEMENTS OF THE STORY

Key-character(s): Willy, teenager
Characters mentioned in the initial-situation: Willy, Mother and older brother.
Other characters mentioned during the telling of the story: Teenager, his brother.

Story-goal of the key-character(s):
- Willy's goal was to enjoy his new car.
- Teenager's goal was to help his crippled brother.

Key-time: Present

Key-location: Large town or small city

Key-crisis:
   Teenager brings his brother to see Willy's car.

Key-repetitions:
- Life was hard.
- Willy was wrong about teenager.
- Willy's new car was a gift that didn't cost him.

Key-attitudes:
- Willy's joy over new car
- Teenager's fascination with Willy's new car
- Teenager's desire to give to his brother

STRUCTURE OF THE STORY

Initial-situation:
   Life was hard for Willy, his mother and brother.

Initial-problem:
   Positive life changing circumstances: Willy's brother signs to play pro-football.

Sequence of events:
- Life had been hard for Willy's family.
- Willy's older brother signed a contract to play pro-football and bought a house for his mother.
- When Willy was a senior in high school, his brother bought him a new car for Christmas.
- Unnamed teenager admires Willy's new car. Willy tells him it's a gift from his brother.
- Teenager surprises Willy when he said, "Wow, I wish I could be a brother like that!"
- Willy offered the teenager a ride.
- Teenager wanted to go by his home.
- Willy thought he wanted to impress family and neighbors.

- However, teenager wanted to show his crippled brother the car.
- Teenager told brother, "Someday I wanna give you a car."
- Friendship began between Willy and the two brothers.
- Willy realized the blessing of giving.

Final-situation:
Willy realized, "It's good to receive gifts. But, blessed is the generous person who delights in giving to others. Willy remembered Christmas was the time to celebrate God's giving his son to the world. Baby Jesus grew into a man who taught, "It is more blessed to give than to receive" (Acts 20:35).

STORY:

Life had been hard for Willy. Before he was born, his father left home. His mother put in long hours working as a waitress to provide for Willy and his older brother. Willy's older brother protected him and became a high school football hero. Then he became a college football star.

Willy's older brother signed a contract to play pro-football. The first thing the football player bought was a house for his mother and brother Willy. The year Willy was a senior in high school, his football playing brother bought him a new fancy car as a Christmas gift.

Willy drove his fancy new car to town. When Willy came out of a store, he saw a teenager admiring his fancy new car. Willy looked at the teenager's faded patched clothes and could identify with the fact that life had been hard for the teenager.

Willy opened the door to his new car and the teenager asked, "Man, is this your car?"
Willy replied, "Yea, my brother gave it to me for Christmas."
The teenager asked, "You mean he gave it to you and it cost you nothing?"
Willy repeated, "Yea, my brother gave it to me for Christmas."
The teenager said, "Wow, I wish..."

Willy thought he knew what the teenager was going to say. He had heard it many times, "Wow, I wish I had a brother like that."

Willy was wrong because the teenager said, "Wow, I wish I could be a brother like that!"

Willy was so amazed at the teenager's answer that he asked him, "Wanna go for a ride in my new car?"

The teenager answered, "Wow, man, I'd love to."

After a short ride, the teenager had a grin on his face and asked Willy, "Man, would you drive down my street?"

Willy smiled to himself; he thought that the teenager wanted to impress his friends and family with the fact that he had a friend with a fancy new car who would give him a ride. However, Willy had again misjudged the teenager.

The teenager shouted, "Stop! Wait just a minute." Then he ran into his home. Willy heard him slowly returning and saw him pushing a younger brother in a wheelchair.

The teenager pushed his brother to the car, touched it and told him, "That's the guy I was telling you about. His brother gave him a new car as a Christmas gift. He has a new car and it didn't cost him a thing. Someday I wanna give you a new car. But, it will be different from this. You'll drive your car with just your hands."

Willy asked the crippled brother, "Wanna go for a ride?" Willy got out of his car and lifted the crippled brother into the passenger seat. The older brother got into the back seat. Willy felt great joy as he gave them a ride around town and out into the country. That was the beginning of a long friendship between Willy and the two brothers.

Willy realized, "It's good to receive gifts. But, blessed is the generous person who delights in giving to others. Willy remembered Christmas was the time to celebrate God's giving his son to the world. Baby Jesus grew into a man who taught, "It is more blessed to give than to receive" (Acts 20:35).

DIGESTION HELPS
Listeners' Participating Activities

After eating, food is digested. Digestion converts bites of food into simpler chemical compounds that can be absorbed and assimilated by the body. For instance, digestion breaks down large food molecules to small ones that can be absorbed into the bloodstream.

Worship services that involve listeners participating in activities, help listeners to digest Scripture. Most worship services only provide two kinds of participating activities: singing and listening.

My mother dreamed about my playing the piano. I was in the first grade when Mother took me to a piano teacher. The piano teacher told Mother to wait until my music talents matured before enrolling me in piano lessons. I was in the fifth grade when Mother took me to another piano teacher who told Mother that my music abilities still hadn't developed. I'm still waiting for my music abilities to develop. Two church music directors asked me to please not sing when I was on the platform, because my off-key singing made it difficult for them to sing on key. I pastored one church plant in Brasilia, Brazil, where several members were professional musicians who played in the famous National Presidential Band. Those professional musicians would not sit close to me at church because my off-key singing irritated them. Recently a musician suggested, "Jack, during the song service, silently mouth, 'Watermelon, watermelon, watermelon,' while others are singing. That way, you'll give the impression that you're singing, but your off-key singing will not irritate those people surrounding me who were blessed with musical talent." My wife has suggested that I mouth the words to the song as others sing it.

I don't have the opportunity to sing in the choir. I've never been invited to sing a solo. My experience inspires me to suggest that churches find activities, beyond singing for non-musical people to participate.

People learn more effectively by doing – by experience. Many churches limit participation to congregational singing and listening. In many churches, only church staff and leaders pray in the worship service. Only the most talented sing in the choir. Many worship services are similar to a performance that the congregation watches.

Multi-sensory preaching uses activities such as props, drama, video clips, object lessons, art, music, thematic backdrops, food, smells and other creative elements. All the senses are information receptors that act as antennas, which receive information. Then the senses become output antennas that transmit information to the brain for processing, learning, and acting. The preacher needs to develop multi-sensory communication activities. Multi-sensory activities interface with multiple senses. Unlike conventional worship which stimulates only the mouth to sing and the ears to hear, multi-sensory communication stimulates multiple senses: that is, the senses of hearing, seeing, touching, and sometimes even smell and taste.

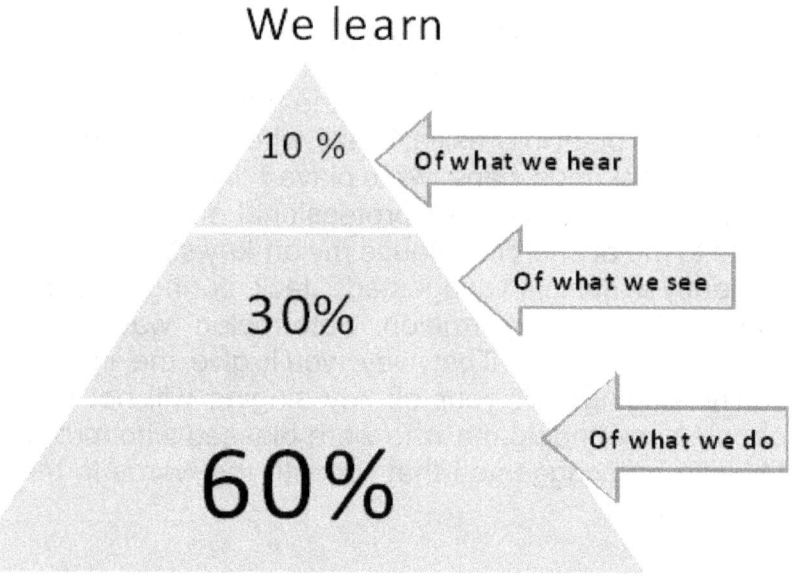

The learning pyramid is often used in courses for training teachers. The training pyramid shows the value of participating in the educational process. We learn 10% of what we hear; 30%

of what we see; and 60% of what we do. It's also valid for showing how participating helps listeners digest Scripture.

The storyteller-preacher wants his listeners to think through the Bible story so they will understand it, absorb it into their thinking and assimilate it into their actions. The following participating activities help listeners experience Bible stories. These activities create an environment that allows listeners to interact to the telling of a Bible story. People remember what they participate in. They help story-listeners to experience the story. Just as chewing food helps digest it, these activities help listeners digest Bible stories.

INTERACTIVE LISTENERS' ACTIVITIES

1. Listen to the Story

I lived on a farm during my childhood. I was twelve years old before I first saw TV. Before TV, our family often gathered at night to listen to a radio drama. Radio drama depended on dialogue, music and sound effects to help us listeners imagine the characters and story. I listened to the radio drama and put myself inside the story with my imagination.

The storytelling-preacher should tell the Bible story as accurately as possible. Tell the story in the past tense. That is the way it is recorded in the Bible. Many literate communicators assume the listeners know the story, so they only summarize the Bible story. A summary loses many characteristics of a story that hold listeners' attention.

When storytelling, just tell the story! Don't tell what the story means; don't interpret the story; don't add insights about the story. Just tell the Bible story. Trust the Bible story to speak to listeners instead of depending on the storytelling-preacher's interpretations.

Tell the story; don't read it. Few people can hold their listeners' attention while reading a story. Tell the story. Also, ask the listeners to close their Bibles and listen to the story. Listeners who read the Bible story while someone is telling it don't get inside the story as much as listeners who imagine the story in their minds as they listen. Both storyteller and listeners should travel together on a story-journey.

2. Story repeated by a listener

The storyteller narrates the Bible story, then he asks for a volunteer listener to repeat the story. Sometimes, a volunteer repeats the story shortly after hearing it. Or, the story may be repeated at the beginning of the next storytelling session.

Often missionaries who are storytelling to oral communicators who are unfamiliar with Bible stories do the following:

1st Storyteller tells the Bible story.
2nd Storyteller repeats the Bible story a second time.
3rd Storyteller asks for a volunteer listener to repeat the story.

3. Dialogue about the story

Tell the Bible story in chronological order; then discuss it with listeners. Asking questions about a story is one key to getting listeners to interact with the story.

Generic questions help create discussion. Generic questions are open questions that can be asked about any Bible story.

The storyteller should allow listeners to do most of the talking. Give listeners freedom to talk about whatever they desire, as long as their discussion is in some way related to the Bible story.

Examples of generic questions:
1) What did you like best about the story?
2) Who are the main characters in the story?
3) What problems did the characters face?
4) How did the characters face their problems?
5) Have you faced similar problems?
6) Is there someone in the story who is similar to you or who is different from you?

7) What life-lessons did you get from the story?
8) What does the story tell about God?
9) Is there anything in the story that is hard to understand?
10) Is there something about the story you want to talk about?

4. Utilize visual aids

It is said that a picture is worth a thousand words. Listeners have a higher level of attention, comprehension and retention when preachers use visual aids. Utilize pictures, video clips, graphic art, objects, projector and screen, or other visual aids.

- *Example*: If preaching on the healing of the paralytic lowered through the roof (Matthew 9:1-8), a picture of a house from the time of Jesus with a flat roof and steps on the outside would help the story be better understood.

- *Example*: For a sermon on spiritual warfare from 1 Corinthians 5:17, the sermon could begin with a video clip from a movie about war. Then the preacher could enter the pulpit dressed in military fatigues.

- *Example*: A pastor visited his church members at work and took pictures of them working. On the Sunday before Labor Day, selected pictures were projected on the screen during the prelude and some were used during the sermon.

- *Example*: A crown of thorns could be displayed while telling the story of Jesus' crucifixion.

The modern video projector and screen can be used as the modern-day version of the old classroom blackboard. The preacher can prepare slide shows with words, diagrams, graphic art, pictures, and sermon outline; then, during his sermon, project the images on a screen.

5. Utilize sound effects

Sounds other than words communicate. Sound effects can be recorded and used during the sermon. Examples would include the sound of a siren, children playing, traffic, birds singing, a storm, the alarm clock, construction work, the ringing of cell phones, a teenager playing a video game, a car motor that won't start, or footsteps coming nearer. Use a specific sound when it will help communicate a biblical truth.

6. Plan interaction activity

The preacher creates an environment where there is interaction between the preacher and his listeners. The worship experience at the church at Corinth was an interactive experience where different people participated. "What then shall we say, brothers and sisters? When you come together, each of you has a hymn, or a word of instruction, a revelation, a tongue or an interpretation. Everything must be done so that the church may be built up" (1 Corinthians 14:26 NIV).

- *Caution*: The preacher who experiments with interactive activities must emphasize that the Bible is the authoritative word of God. Listeners need to evaluate their life-experiences by God's Word instead of evaluating Bible stories by their own personal experiences.

The preacher can ask questions or suggest activities that invite the listeners to interact with the Bible story. The preacher wants listeners to share stories that help them understand and experience the Scripture. Beware of asking questions for listeners to share their opinions or answer purely on a detached, intellectual level. Look for questions that explore feelings, experiences, stories, and images. Ask life-experience questions.

- *Example*: Tell the story of Jesus healing the paralytic lowered through the roof (Matthew 9:1-8). Then ask, "What would you like to say to the characters in this story: to Jesus? to the men who carried the paralytic man? to the religious leaders who criticized Jesus in their thoughts? Tell us what you would like to say to them."

- *Example*: At Christmas time, a pastor asked mothers to share with the congregation their inner thoughts during pregnancy. Then the pastor mentioned that these women "pondered in their hearts" just as Mary did.
- *Example*: Before preaching on Jesus' Gethsemane experience, a preacher asked a couple of people to share: "What was the hardest thing you ever faced in your life?"
- *Example*: A preacher told the Parable of the Good Samaritan (Luke 10:25-37) and asked if anyone who had suffered an experience of being wounded and abandoned would share who most helped them.
- *Example*: One preacher encouraged listeners to text questions during the sermon. After the sermon, selected questions were projected on the screen for the pastor to answer.
- *Example*: One preacher allows listeners on the Wednesday night gathering to ask him questions about his previous Sunday sermon.

7. Pray back the story

Ask listeners to talk to God about the story. Invite them to tell God:
- How they feel about the story.
- How they are similar or different than characters in the story.
- What decisions they need to make as a result of hearing the story.
- How their life-issues are similar or different than the characters in the story.
- How the story helps them face personal life-issues.
- How the story helps them better know God.

8. Utilize a chant

Craft a chant of the core message of a Bible story, or Scripture verse(s). Separate the verse(s) or story into two parts that can be vocalized back and forth by two groups. Words that are to be stressed as focal words are **bold and underlined**.

Include a final part that will be vocalized by all chanters and listeners.

Instructions: Divide the participants into two groups. The first group reads the first part and the second group reads a response. Stress as focal words the ones that are **bold and underlined**. The best way to emphasize a word is to prolong and stretch it out. Stress the word by length, not by volume. Continue switching back and forth as indicated in the chant. Conclude with the final part that will be vocalized by all chanters and listeners.

Example # 1: **Story's Core Message** (Genesis 1)

ALL: "God saw all that he had made, and it was very good" (Genesis 1:31 NIV).	
GROUP 1	**GROUP 2**
In the **beginning**...	God **created** the heavens and the earth.
The first day, God created **light**.	God saw that it was **good**.
The second day, God **separated** waters...	Waters **under** the sky from waters **above** the sky.
The third day, God **gathered** waters into the ocean, and dry land appeared.	And God created **plants**, including trees and grain.
The fourth day, God **created lights** to appear in the sky...	The sun, the moon and the stars.
The fifth day, God created creatures to **swim** in the water, and birds to **fly** over dry land.	And God saw that it was **good**.
The sixth day God created **animals**...	Tame animals, wild animals, and reptiles.
God also created **humans** to be like him...	Like him, and to **rule** the fish, the birds and other creatures.
The seventh day, God **rested**.	He rested from his creation work.
ALL: "God saw all that he had made, and it was very good" (Genesis 1:31 NIV).	

Example # 2: **Scripture That Relates to Life-lesson Found in Story**

STORYTELLER: A core truth of Joseph's story in the Old Testament is found in the New Testament, Romans 8:28.	
GROUP 1	**GROUP 2**
And we **know**.	Yes, we **know** for sure.
In all things, God works for the **good**.	Not **all** things are good. Some things are **evil**.
In all things, God **works** for the good.	Is this always true?
In all things, God works for the good of those who **love** him.	Who love him.
In all things, God works for the good of those who have been **called** according to his purpose.	Who have been chosen for **his purpose**.
All CHANTERS AND ALL LISTENERS	
"And we know that in all things God works for the good of those who love him, who have been called according to his purpose" (Romans 8:28 NIV).	

9. **Music**

    - Create a song that goes with the Bible story or Scripture text. Many groups have people with musical ability who can come up with a rhyme that relates to the Bible story or text and put it to music. Often someone can create a song with both words and melody. Other times they can make up words for a melody they already know.
    - Find a song that is about the Bible story. There are many songs that relate to Bible stories.
      Examples: "Zacchaeus Was a Wee Little Man," (Luke 19:1-10) or "The Wise Man Built His House upon the Rock" (Matthew 7:24-29).
    - Find a song that relates to a life-lesson found in the story.
      Example: The secular song, "Three Wooden Crosses" could relate to the story Rahab the Prostitute (Joshua 2:1-21; 6:22-23). The song repeatedly mentions "three wooden crosses on the right side of the highway." The

song describes four passengers on a bus that was involved in a fatal accident which kills three passengers: a farmer, a teacher, and a preacher. As the preacher was dying, he laid his bloodstained Bible in the hands of a hooker. The end of the song reveals that the story was being told by a preacher during Sunday church services. The preacher is the son of the hooker who received the bloodstained Bible.
- Play over the sound system a recorded song that relates to the Bible story while a projector shows scenes that relate to the words of the song.

10. Arts and crafts

The first gift of the Holy Spirit was the gift of artistic craftsmanship given to Bezalel. God's Spirit filled Bezalel with skill, ability and knowledge in all kinds of crafts so he could make the Tabernacle and its furnishings (Exodus 35:30-33).

Participants with artistic ability can paint a picture of a scene within the Bible story. The person gifted with craft making can make something that connects to the story.
- *Example*: a craftsman can make a shepherd's staff to represent the staff Moses used, or an animal feeding trough to represent baby Jesus in the manger.
- *Example*: I once preached on Mount Up with Wings of an Eagle (Isaiah 40:28-31). A photographer shared a picture he had taken of an eagle soaring, and it was projected onto a screen during the entire sermon.
- *Example*: An artist can paint a picture related to the sermon while the preacher is preaching.

Many people with art and craft abilities could never teach a Bible study, could not sing in public, and some would not even pray in public; but they could gladly craft a project that helps communicate a Bible story.

11. Pantomime

To pantomime is to communicate by means of gestures and facial expressions. To pantomime a story is to tell the story without speaking words, but by means of body movements, gestures, and facial expressions.

- <u>Echo pantomime</u>. First, the storyteller pantomimes a Bible story as he tells it; then he retells the story with listeners joining in and imitating his pantomime actions.

- <u>Listener-created pantomime</u>. The storyteller informs listeners that he will tell the Bible story one time. Then he will repeat the story with volunteers standing in front pantomiming the action as the storyteller narrates the story a second time.

- Have someone who speaks in sign language sign the story as it is being told.

12. Role-playing drama

Tell the Bible story; then ask listeners to spontaneously dramatize it.

A few volunteers can act out the story. Appoint people to act the part of each key-character in the story you just told.
Example:
After telling the story of Adam and Eve's sin in Genesis 3, choose actors to represent:
- Adam
- Eve
- The snake
- God

Have actors say or act out what the character they represent did.

It is possible to involve everyone in the drama. Put everyone on stage.

Example:
After telling the story of Adam and Eve's sin in Genesis 3, choose actors to represent:
- Adam
- Eve
- The snake
- God

Then choose others to have non-speaking roles:
- The Tree of the Knowledge of Good and Evil
- The Tree of Life
- Ask several people to be one of the trees
- Ask several people to be one of the animals

Often spontaneous actors will leave something out or add something to the story. When this happens, thank the actors for their participation. Then ask:
- Was anything left out of the story?
- Was anything added to the story?

Example:
Tell the story of David's adultery with Bathsheba and his having her husband, Uriah, murdered.

Invite two volunteers to role play a part. Give them the following instructions: "I want you to imagine you are two soldiers who have faithfully followed King David. You have just heard what David did to Uriah, Bathsheba's husband. How are you going to react to the news of how David treated Uriah?"

13. Dramatic monologue of story-characters

Tell the Bible story one or two times. Then ask different volunteers to imagine that they were a story-character. Have each volunteer tell the story from the viewpoint of his story-character.

Example:
Tell the story of Jesus Healing the Paralytic Man Lowered Through the Roof (Matthew 9:1-8). Then have several volunteers spontaneously tell the story from the viewpoint of one of the story-characters:
- One of the men who carried the paralytic to Jesus

- A person who stood in the doorway and refused to give up his space so the men who carried the paralytic could enter the house
- Two religious leaders who criticized Jesus
- The owner of the house

14. Tableau

A tableau refers to drama participants making a frozen image with their bodies to represent one scene or event. Drama participants remain motionless and silent as though they were in a painting. A tableau is an effective method for staging a Bible story quickly.

Tableau options:

- **Drama with tableau interludes**. The storyteller narrates the Bible story from beginning until the end. Then the storyteller invites some participants to dramatize the story as he retells it. Whenever the storyteller gives a certain signal, such as saying the word "Freeze" or ringing a bell, all drama participants freeze in position and remain frozen during the tableau interlude. After each tableau interlude, the storyteller resumes his narration and drama participants resume acting out the story as before. The storyteller may have several tableaux or only one.

- **Series of tableaux**. The storyteller narrates the Bible story from beginning until the end. Then drama participants plan a series of frozen images that, together, tell the story with a beginning, middle and end. Each drama participant is designated to represent a thing or person from the story. The storyteller starts retelling the Bible story. Drama participants stand around the performance area. When the storyteller pauses narrating, drama participants interpret the narrated event by stepping into the performance area and establishing a frozen image in relation to one another until the tableau is complete. At this point, "thought tracking" can be used to find out more about each of the characters. The storyteller acts as a reporter and asks drama participants what they are thinking, feeling, or why they chose their frozen position. At the end of the tableau interlude, drama participants resume standing around the performance area and the storyteller resumes narrating the story. The storyteller and drama participants continue in this way after each tableau interlude, until the storyteller completes telling the story.

- **Group tableau collaboration**. The storyteller narrates the Bible story from beginning until the end. Small groups are asked to give suggestions for drama participants to represent a story-scene in a tableau. The storyteller assigns each group a person or thing mentioned in the story. One actor from each group will be creating a frozen image on stage that captures the essence of the assignment. Each group collaborates by giving suggestions to its drama participant on how to craft his gestures, facial expressions and physical poses. Give groups enough time to plan and rehearse. When the groups are ready, drama participants unite to present their tableau scene.

During a tableau interlude, the storyteller could act as a reporter and conduct short interviews with actors in the tableau to interpret the frozen scene. *For example*, the storyteller could ask drama participants what they are thinking, feeling, or why they chose their position.

The storyteller might choose to facilitate a discussion with the audience by highlighting certain tableau details through questioning. *For example*, the storyteller could ask, "Why might this character be smiling?" or "What do you think this character is thinking?"

Example of a tableau:
    1st Tell the story of Jesus' Invitation to Levi (Luke 5:27-32).
    2nd Ask volunteers to dramatize with a frozen image the scene where Jewish religious leaders ask Jesus' disciples "Why do you eat and drink with tax collectors and sinners?" Assign volunteers to represent the following characters in the story:
       Jesus
- Levi (also called Matthew)
- A tax collector

- A woman with a bad reputation, who is a guest at Levi's banquet
- One of Jesus' disciples
- A religious leader

3rd Retell the Bible story of Jesus' Invitation to Levi through the event where Jewish religious leaders asks the disciples, "Why do you eat and drink with tax collectors and sinners?". Then the storyteller stops narrating and drama participants step onto the performance area to interpret the scene by making a frozen image with their bodies.

15. Polymorphic communication

The oral word massages the ear. The written word massages the eye. The electronic media can massage both eye and ear during the same time. The storytelling-preacher can be polymorphic and communicate, utilizing more than one of the senses.

Examples:
- The storyteller tells the story while an actor pantomimes the story as it is being told.
- One pastor preached on Jacob's ladder (Genesis 28:10-22). At the beginning of the worship service, two men dressed in work clothes entered the church carrying a long ladder. They marched down the aisle, onto the pulpit and placed the ladder against the back wall of the church.
- A pastor's text was Galatians 5. His theme was BONDAGE TO SIN OR FREEDOM IN CHRIST. The preacher was beginning his sermon when a police car, with sirens blasting and lights flashing, raced onto the church's parking lot. Deacons rushed to lock the doors; however, the policemen stormed into the church and claimed to be searching for a certain youth. They named the youth and the pastor pointed him out. The policemen handcuffed the youth. The pastor requested for the policemen to sit down and wait until church was over before taking the youth away. The pastor continued his sermon and explained how sin chains a person to

bondage and faith in Christ frees a person to serve God. The pastor asked the youth if he had faith in Jesus. The youth replied "Yes." The policemen removed the handcuffs and the youth stood up on a pew, holding his hands high, and shouted, "I'm free, Christ set me free."
Observation: Before the worship service, the pastor had asked the young man to participate in the drama, and he had warned the boy's parents and people with heart problems that drama would be taking place.

- A storytelling-preacher could tell the story of the Sinful Woman Anointing Jesus with Perfume (Luke 7:36-50). He could arrange for people sitting in different parts of the church to discreetly spray perfumed smelling air freshener as he told the story. Listeners would both hear the story of the woman pouring perfume onto Jesus' feet, and they would sniff the fragrance of perfume.
Caution: Before using a fragrance, such as perfume, make sure no one is allergic to it.
- An artist or chalk artist could paint a picture related to a Bible story while the storytelling-preacher is narrating the story.

WHERE DO STORIES COME FROM?
Sources for Stories

The initial source of most food is the farm. The source of raw food for many cooks is a garden in their back yard. However, most cooks today find food in a grocery store or a farmer's market.

The storytelling-preacher can find many sources for stories.

The preacher needs to develop the habit of searching for stories and making notes to help him remember useful ones.

Stories can be adapted in order to best illustrate a truth. Don't simply use a story the way it was found. Update it, personalize it, and shape it so it best illustrates the biblical truth. However, the preacher must be truthful. He should not recreate biblical stories, nor should he alter historical facts; however, he may condense such stories to mention only details that help illustrate the biblical truth.

Finding stories to illustrate a particular text or theme require looking for stories by observing life, events, and people. It also requires time spent in reading printed material, and time spent in searching on the internet for stories. It also requires commitment of time to organize stories.

The storyteller can find many seed-beds with ideas for stories. I'm going to mention some of the sources for story seed-beds.

1. **Bible stories**

The storytelling-preacher's most obvious source of stories is the Bible itself. The Bible both explains and illustrates itself. The first source in finding illustrations to biblical teaching is the Bible. A Bible story is useful as a text for a sermon. But, Bible stories are also useful to illustrate biblical teachings.

The Bible is not only a theological text; it is a casebook with examples of every kind of moral choice and behavior. The Holy Spirit will use Bible stories told as illustrations, useful for teaching, rebuking, correcting, training in righteousness, and in equipping God's servant for every good work (2 Timothy 3:16-17). The Bible is a treasure book of illustrations.

If the storyteller uses a Bible story, be sure to tell the story. Don't just mention the story or summarize it. Tell the story. Assume that your listeners are unfamiliar with the Bible story and tell it.

2. Personal experiences

Your second source in finding illustrations is your own life. Scan your life and you are sure to find amusing anecdotes and life-defining moments.

Every person who survived childhood has many stories which could be told. Stories that grow out of a storyteller's experiences have a powerful impact. Your personal experience stories make you unique. No one can tell your stories like you can. Even if others may later tell your life story, only you can tell it in the first person. Getting sick, breaking a bone, going to a doctor, getting lost, losing a friend, gaining a new friend, or moving to a new home are all personal experiences. You have unique life-altering experiences that need to be told.

Listeners will receive your message more readily if they realize you aren't perfect. This gives them hope that if you can overcome your failures and limitations, then they too can overcome their failures and limitations.

Personal stories may be the literal truth or they may be events that have been embellished for the sake of a story. Embellished stories may be rearranged and people's names changed in order not to embarrass them. Embellished stories may have several different real characters woven into one story character; different events over a period of several years may be woven into a time frame of a day or a week.

3. Family stories

Almost every family has stories that are told when the relatives gather. They are stories of the doings of certain family members or events that happened to them. Recall stories told by your parents and grandparents. Recall stories about your parents. Recall some of the things you did with your siblings and other family members. If you are married, you have some stories to tell about your mate, children, and in-laws.

4. Personal relationships

Every personal relationship is a seed-bed for one or more stories, such as:
- Boyfriend with girlfriend
- Husband with wife
- Friend with friend
- Boss with employee
- Co-worker with co-worker
- Enemies
- Teammates

5. Country music

Much of country music is story put to song. Country music is popular because it gives voice to what many people are feeling, experiencing, and thinking. The preacher who illustrates with country music will share a story that is relevant to his listeners' lives.

6. Crisis experiences

Crisis experiences catch listeners' attention quicker than good experiences. Examples of crisis experiences:
- Failing a grade in school
- Getting fired
- Experiencing the death of a loved one
- Getting arrested
- Being responsible for losing a game
- Dealing with a child's arrest
- Dealing with a child who is addicted to drugs

7. Embarrassing events

Listeners love to hear about embarrassing events. Examples of embarrassing events:
- Forgetting an appointment
- Knocking a dish over, falling, or dropping things at a formal dinner
- Being unaware that you were to speak at a meeting until you entered the door and received a bulletin that listed you as the key speaker
- Being advised to dress casually, and you showed up in Bermuda shorts. However, the other men showed up wearing casual dress pants, sport jackets and ties
- Finding your name on the front page of the newspaper, because a person whose name is the same as yours has committed a crime

8. Observation

One of the best ways to find stories is simple observation. Observe events and things that arouse your emotions. Observe all life – people, events, places, objects, situations or conversations. You can discover stories, anecdotes, and illustrations as much from observing nature and inanimate objects such as buildings, as you can from watching people. A news story, an incident, a casual remark in a conversation among friends, or even with strangers, can all provide inspiration for a story that can form material for your sermon.

The storyteller needs to look at life as a photographer looks through a camera, constantly framing a moment, an event, people and experiences. What is common to the ordinary eye is significant to the photographer. Storytelling-preachers need to continually take story snapshots of both life's great experiences and commonplace experiences. Learn to see in the ordinary that which illustrates life-lessons and scriptural truths. There are no insignificant people, events, places, jobs or conversations for the storytelling-preacher. All have the potential for helping you communicate God's Word. Most ideas in their infancy are flawed, silly, or ridiculous. However, they are story-seeds that can grow into powerful stories. So, if something catches your attention, make a note of it. If you don't, you may struggle to recall the details later.

9. Listen

Listen to people talking and observe the stories they tell. I've heard some interesting stories while sitting on a mall bench waiting for my wife to finish her shopping, or overhearing people talk while I'm sitting in an airport waiting room, or overhearing people who are sitting at a nearby table at a restaurant. Listen to public speakers, politicians, and preachers. Make notes on story-ideas that could illustrate biblical truths.

10. Read

Newspapers provide current illustrations.

In literature, the storyteller finds stories written by an author for the purpose of publication. Be an avid reader and devour written stories. Copyright laws may prohibit you from telling a written story verbatim. If you tell a published story, be sure to respect copyrights and give credit to the original author. However, literature can be most helpful in giving you seed-ideas for crafting original stories. A situation or event you find in literature may give you an idea for a story or anecdote.

11. World of art

Wonderful stories can be discovered from novels, movies, drama, popular songs and television. Expressions of culture reveal to us the worldview of our time. Popular works of art are popular because they give voice to what many people are feeling and thinking. The preacher who illustrates with works of art will share a story that is relevant to his listeners' lives.

12. History

Many interesting people lived in the past and stories about them can illustrate biblical truths and relate to today's listeners.

13. Internet

The storytelling-preacher can use the internet to find stories. *Example*: The preacher who needs a story to illustrate greed can do an internet search for: "Story, greed." He will find a listing of multiple web sites with stories about greed.

You can sign up for a service such as Google Alerts, so that you are notified of news stories that relate to your subject matter. You need to select your key words and choose how often you wish to receive alerts. You will then have an automatic way to keep abreast of the latest news stories on topics that you will be preaching about and you will have fresh material to incorporate into your sermon.

14. Library

The table below gives information on the Dewey Decimal numbers to help you find stories in your public library. Your library may use different numbering; so if you can't find something, ask your librarians for help.

292	Greek and Roman mythology
372	Reading education. Some books on storytelling
398.2	Folktales, fairy tales and other narratives
808.87-.88	Toasts, jokes and stories for public speakers
810	American literature
817 818	These sections include diverse literary offerings that include short stories and collections of humor
823	English literature
920s	Biographies. Biographies are arranged by the last name of the person whose life is the subject of the biography
B-O-ED	Recordings of books and stories

*****

Finding illustrations are like finding crystals in a mountainous creek bottom in an area known for limestone. Crystals are all around the creek bed; however, it takes finding a few crystals yourself before your eyes begin to recognize rocks that hold the sparkling treasure within. Unless you walk the creek bank looking for crystals, all you see in the creek bottom is an endless supply of indistinguishable rocks. The preacher must train his eyes and ears to look for stories in ordinary situations.

The first rule to finding good stories is simple: Become a collector of stories. Develop a story-searching mentality. Always be on the outlook for stories. Keep your story antennae up. The one who starts looking for good stories will find them everywhere and soon will experience story-ideas popping into his mind.

RECORD AND KEEP STORY-IDEAS

The storytelling-preacher needs to acquire the habit of recording and preserving story-ideas. He needs to search for stories and make notes to help him remember useful ones. A person should put money into savings so he will have money in time of need. The preacher who saves an abundance of story-ideas will be able to find a story for a special occasion, or to illustrate a biblical truth.

There are books of illustrations; however, the preacher will find it more gratifying to find his own illustrations.

If you like a story, save it. Save it in the computer or jot it down and save the paper. The shortest stubby pencil is better than the longest memory. Write down anecdotes and stories that could be used to illustrate biblical teaching.

Stories come from many sources. However, if the storytelling-preacher does not record and keep story-ideas, he will forget most of them. I always have 3X5 note cards in my shirt pocket so I can jot down story-ideas and later record them in my computer. I also have a story-idea box where I throw clippings from newspapers, magazines, e-mails and letters. I usually look through the box about every six months.

The important thing is to have a system for recording and keeping story-ideas. Record and keep notes on what you experience, see, hear, and feel; and record ideas about using them in a story or sermon. If something interests you, it has the seed for a story that will interest others.

Often several years pass between the time I note a story-idea and the time when I finally craft the idea into a story. I wonder how many story-ideas were lost because I did not write them down and keep them for future reference. Almost any system of collecting and filing story-ideas is better than no system at all. No filing system will work if you don't write it down and save it. Many times I've thought of a good story-idea to illustrate a biblical teaching, but I failed to write it down. Later, I racked my brain to remember the story-idea, but most of the time my memory failed me and the idea was gone.

CONCLUSION

Preachers today are living in a time of change of cultural communication. For the first time since the invention of the alphabet and manuscript, a new form of communication has become more powerful than the written word. Electronic communication has changed our world by becoming more powerful than the written word. Preachers today are living in the time of the greatest change of cultural communication since the formation of the church. This is the first time in the history of Christianity in which the most powerful medium of cultural communication is not writing. Electronic communication uses oral-visual storytelling. The preacher needs to learn the language of storytelling to communicate to today's culture.

Nearly all Scripture, from Genesis to Revelation, flows with narrative and story. More than 70% of the Bible is in story form. Abraham's descendants were storytellers who told God's stories. God's historical acts are set in the framework of stories. Jesus perfected communicating God's message in story. He told stories, called parables, every time he spoke. The early church was a storytelling community. The early church's typical order of worship was: gather people, tell stories, and break bread. A return to biblical roots requires a return to storytelling. The storytelling-preacher comes closer to gospel language than any other literary or oral communication form.

It is my prayer that this book helps preachers imitate Jesus by speaking in story. As a result, I pray that the preacher's listeners will find the connection between biblical events and day-to-day events in their own lives. May this book help you tell Bible stories so your listeners will hear the greatest story ever told. May this book help you imitate Jesus by telling stories to put people on the road to truth. As you tell stories, may all your listeners hear good stories; may those who are spiritually sensitive hear a word from God.

LIST OF BIBLE STORIES IN CHRONOLOGICAL ORDER

The **List of Bible Stories in Chronological Order** is an adaptation of a list from the book ***Bible Storytelling Tools***, by the same author, Jackson Day.

This list should help storytelling-preachers find the text for a story in the Bible.

List of Bible Stories with References	Text
1. Old Testament Stories	
Creation	Genesis 1, 2
First Sin	3:1-24
Cain and Abel	4:1-10
Flood	6:1-9:17
Tower of Babel	11:1-9
God Calls Abram	12:1-5
Abram and Lot Separate	13:1-13
God's Covenant with Abram	15:1-21; 17:1-27; 18:1-15
Hagar and Ishmael	16:1-15; 21:8-20
Sodom and Gomorrah Destroyed, Lot after Sodom	18:16- 19:38
Isaac's Birth - Abraham Tested, Rebekah	21-24
Jacob, Esau, and Laban	26 -31
Joseph the Slave	37 - 41
Joseph, Governor in Egypt	41:41 - 45
Jacob and Family in Egypt	46 - 50
Joseph Forgives His Brothers	45:1-15; 50:15-21
Moses' Birth, Moses the Young Man	Exodus 1 - 2
God Calls Moses to Return to Egypt	3:1 - 4:31
Moses and Pharaoh, Plagues 1-9	5 - 10
Passover and Exodus from Egypt	11- 12
Crossing the Sea	13:17 - 14:31
Bitter Water	15:22-27
God Provides Manna, Quail and Water	16 - 17
War Against the Amalekites	17:8-16

List of Bible Stories with References	Text
Jethro Counsels Moses	18:1-27
Mount Sinai, the Ten Commandments	19 - 20
Golden Calf	32:1-35
Making the Tabernacle	35 - 40
Death of Nadab and Abihu	Leviticus 10:1-5
Miriam and Aaron Oppose Moses	Numbers 12
Spies with Little Faith	13:1-2, 17-33
Israelites Murmur, Must Wander in the Desert	14:1-45
Budding of Aaron's Staff	17
Moses Strikes the Rock at Meribah	20:2-13
Bronze Snake	21:4-9
Balaam and the Speaking Donkey	22 - 24
Worship of Baal, Peor and the Zeal of Phinehas	25:1-18
Midianites Destroyed, the Transjordan Tribes	31 - 32
Joshua Replaces Moses	Joshua 1:1-9
Rahab and the Spies in Jericho	2:1-21
Crossing the Jordan	3 - 4
Conquest of Jericho	6:1-27
Achan's Sin	7:1-26
Joshua Deceived by the Gibeonites	9:1-26
Victories of Joshua	10 - 12
Joshua's Farewell	23 - 24
Israelites Abandon God	Judges 2:6 - 3:6
Deborah and Barak	4 - 5
Gideon	6 - 8
Samson	13 -16
Ruth	Ruth 1 - 4
Hannah's Prayer and Samuel's Birth	1 Samuel 1:1 - 2:11
Eli and His Sons	2:12-36; 4:12-22
God Speaks to the Boy Samuel	3:1-14
Philistines and the Ark of the Covenant	4:1 - 7:1
Samuel Governs Israel	7:2-17
Saul Becomes King	8 - 11

List of Bible Stories with References	Text
Samuel's Farewell Speech	12
Saul's Mistakes	13 - 15; 28, 31
Samuel Anoints David; David in Saul's Service	16:1-23
David and Goliath	17:1-54
David and Jonathan	1 Sam 18:1-5; 20:1-43; 2 Sam 9
David Fleeing from Saul	1 Sam 19 - 31
David Becomes King	2 Samuel 1 - 5
God's Covenant with David	7:1-29
David's Victories	5, 8, 10
David's Sin with Bathsheba; David Rebuked by Nathan	11, 12
Amnon and Tamar	13:1-22
Absalom	13:23 - 19:43
Solomon Becomes King	1 Kings 1 - 2
Solomon's Wisdom	3:1-28; 10:1-13
Solomon Builds the Temple	5:13 - 8:66
Solomon: Faithful to God	1 - 10
Solomon: Unfaithful to God	11:1-43
Division of the Kingdom: Judah and Israel	12:1-24
Idolatry of King Jeroboam in Israel	12:16-33
Prophet Elijah; King Ahab and Queen Jezebel	1 Kn 17 - 22; 2 Kn 9:30-37
Elijah and Baal's Prophets on Mount Carmel	1 Kn 18:17-46
Elijah Flees Jezebel; Mt Horeb; Call of Elisha	19:1-21
Ahab Takes Naboth's Vineyard	21:1-29
Soldiers Killed by Fire	2 Kings 1:1-16
Elijah Taken to Heaven	2:1-18
Prophet Elisha	1 Kn 19:19-21; 2 Kn 2 - 13
Elisha Purifies Water	2 Kn 2:19-22
Elisha Multiplies the Widow's Oil	4:1-7
Elisha Restores a Boy to Life	4:8-37
Naaman Healed of Leprosy	5:1-27
Elisha Makes an Axhead Float	6:1-7

List of Bible Stories with References	Text
Jonah	Jonah 1 - 4
Fall of Israel	2 Kings 17:1-41
King Hezekiah of Judah	18:13- 20:21
Isaiah's Vision and Vocation	Isaiah 6:1-9
King Josiah of Judah	2 Kings 22:23-30
Conquest of Judah; Exile into Babylon	2 Kn 24:18 - 25:22
Daniel's Education	Daniel 1:1-21
King Nebuchadnezzar's Dream; Daniel Interprets the Dream	2:1-49
Daniel's Friends; the Image of Gold and the Fiery Furnace	3:1-31
King Nebuchadnezzar Lives as a Wild Animal	4:1-37
Writing on the Wall	5:1-30
Daniel in the Lions' Den	6:1-28
Ezra: Exiles Return to Jerusalem; Rebuilding the Temple	Ezra 1 - 10
Nehemiah: Rebuilding the Walls for Jerusalem	Nehemiah 1 - 13
Esther	Esther 1 - 10
2. Stories from the Life of Jesus	Matthew; Mark; Luke; John
2.1 Jesus' Birth and Childhood	
Birth of John the Baptist Foretold	Lk 1:5-25
Mary Foretold of Jesus' Birth	Lk 1:26-38
Mary Visits Elizabeth	Lk 1:39-56
Joseph Was Foretold of Jesus' Birth	Mt 1:18-25
Birth of John the Baptist	Lk 1:57-80
Birth of Jesus Christ	Lk 2:1-7
Shepherds of Bethlehem	Lk 2:8-20
Jesus Presented in the Temple	Lk 2:22-38
Visit of the Wise Men	Mt 2:1-12
Escape to Egypt; Childhood in Nazareth	Mt 2:13-18
Boy Jesus at the Temple	Lk 2:41-50
2.2 First Year of Public Ministry; the Year of Preparation	
John the Baptist Prepares for Jesus	Mt 3:1-11; Lk 3:1-18
Baptism of Jesus	Mt 3:13-17

List of Bible Stories with References	Text
Temptation of Jesus	Mt 4:1-11; Lk 4:1-13
First Disciples	Jn 1:29-51
Water Transformed into Wine	Jn 2:1-11
First Cleansing of the Temple	Jn 2:13-22
Jesus with Nicodemus	Jn 3:1-21
Jesus with the Samaritan Woman	Jn 4:4-42
Jesus Heals the Official's Son from a Distance	Jn 4:46-54
2.3 Second Year of Public Ministry; the Year of Popularity	
John the Baptist Imprisoned; Jesus Preaches in Galilee	Mt 4:12-17
Jesus Rejected at Nazareth	Lk 4:16-30
Jesus Calls Four Fishermen	Mt 4:18-22; Lk 5:1-11
Simon Peter's Mother-in-law Healed	Mk 1:29-33
Calling of Matthew/Levi	Mt 9:9-13; Lk 5:27-32
Parables in Defense of His Disciples Who Did Not Fast	Mt 9:14-17; Mk 2:18-22; Lk 5:33-39
Healing of the Invalid at Pool on Sabbath	Jn 5:1-47
Jesus Defends His Disciples Who Picked Grain on the Sabbath	Mt 12:1-8; Mk 2:23-28; Lk 6:1-5
Jesus Heals a Man with a Shriveled Hand on the Sabbath	Mt 12:9-14; Mk 3:1-6; Lk 6:6-11
Jesus Selects Twelve Disciples	Mk 3:13-19; Lk 6:12-16
Sermon on the Mountain	Mt 5, 6, 7
Centurion's Faith; His Servant Healed	Mt 8:5-13; Lk 7:1-10
Jesus Restores the Widow's Son to Life	Lk 7:11-17
John the Baptist Asks; Jesus Answers	Mt 11:1-19; Lk 7:18-35
Sinful Woman Anoints Jesus; Parable: Two Debtors	Lk 7:36-50
Blasphemy of the Pharisees; Unforgivable Sin	Mt 12:22-37; Mk 3:20-30
Jesus' Mother and Brothers	Mk 3:21, 31-34
Parables about Growth in the Kingdom of God	Mt 13:3-53; Mk 4:3-34; Lk 8:5-25
Jesus Calms Storm on a Lake	Mt 8:23-27; Mk 4:35-41; Lk 8:22-25
Healing of Two Demon-possessed Men	Mt 8:28-34; Mk 5:1-20; Lk 8:26-39

List of Bible Stories with References	Text
Dead Girl Resurrected; Sick Woman Healed	Mt 9:18-26; Mk 5:21-43; Lk 8:40-56
Jesus Instructs and Sends out the Twelve	Mt 10:1-16; Mk 6:7-13; Lk 9:1-6
Herod Kills John the Baptist	Mt 14:1-12; Mk 6:14-29
2.4 Third Year of Public Ministry; the Year of Opposition	
2.4.1 Semester of Retreats; a Time of Special Instruction for the Twelve	
5,000 Fed from Five Loaves and Two Fish	Mk 6:34-44; Jn 6:4-14
Jesus Walks on Water	Mk 6:47-52; Jn 6:16-21
Jesus the Bread of Life; Many Disciples Desert Him	Jn 6:25-71
Jesus Disputes with the Pharisees about Traditions	Mt 15:1-20; Mk 7:1-23
Daughter of a Syrophoenician Woman Healed	Mt 15:21-28; Mk 7:24-30
4,000 Fed	Mt 15:32-39; Mk 8:1-10
Blind Cured	Mk 8:22-26
Pharisees and Sadducees Demand a Sign	Mt 15:39 - 16:4
Peter's Confession	Mt 16:13-20; Mk 8:27-30; Lk 9:18-20
Jesus Predicts His Death; Peter's Reprimand	Mt 16:21-28; Mk 8:31-9:1; Lk 9:22-27
Transfiguration	Mt 17:1-13; Mk 9:2-13; Lk 9:28-36
Demon-possessed Boy Healed	Mt 17:14-21: Mk 9:14-29; Lk 9:37-43
Temple Tax; Coin in the Fish's Mouth	Mt 17:24-27
Greatest in the Kingdom of Heaven	Mt 18:1-35; Mk 9:33-50
The Cost of Following Jesus	Mt 18:19-22; Lk 9:57-62
2.4.2 Semester of Encounters in Jerusalem	
Jesus Rejects Advice from His Unbelieving Brothers	Jn 7:1-10
Rejection in a Samaritan Village	Lk 9:51-56
Jesus at the Feast of Tabernacles	Jn 7:11-52
An Adulteress Brought to Jesus for Judgment	Jn 8:1-11

List of Bible Stories with References	Text
Jesus Argues with Pharisees about Validity of His Testimony	Jn 8:12-58
Man Born Blind Healed on Sabbath; Parable of Good Shepherd	Jn 9:1 - 10:21
Mission of the Seventy	Lk 10:1-24
Parable: Good Samaritan	Lk 10:25-37
Martha and Mary Visited	Lk 10:38-41
Jesus Accused of Being in League with Beelzebub	Lk 11:14-36
Jesus Pronounces Six Woes on Pharisees	Lk 11:37-54
Parable: Rich Fool	Lk 12:16-21
Crippled Woman Healed on Sabbath	Lk 13:10-17
Jesus at Feast of Dedication; Unbelief of the Jews	Jn 10:22-42
At Pharisee's House; Parables: Honor, Great Banquet	Lk 14:1-24
Cost of Being a Disciple	Lk 14:15-35
Parables: Things Lost and Found–Sheep, Coin, and Son	Lk 15:1-31
Parables on Stewardship: Unjust Steward; Rich Man and Lazarus	Lk 16
Teaching and Parable: Sin and Forgiveness	Lk 17:1-10
Lazarus Raised from Dead	Jn 11:1-44
Ten Healed of Leprosy; Grateful Samaritan	Lk 17:11-19
Parables on Prayer: Persistent Widow; Pharisee and Publican	Lk 18:19-14
Jesus Teaches Concerning Divorce	Mt 19:1-12; Mk 10:1-12
Jesus and the Little Children	Mt 19:13-15; Mk 10:13-16; Lk 18:15-17
Rich Young Ruler	Mt 19:16-29; Mk 10:17-31; Lk 18:18-30
Parable: Workers in the Vineyard	Mt 20:1-16
Selfish Request of James and John	Mt 20:20-28; Mk 10:35-45
Blind Bartimaeus and Companion Healed	Mt 20:29-34; Mk 10:46-52; Lk 18:35-43
Jesus and Zacchaeus	Lk 19:1-10
Parable: 10 Minas of Gold	Lk 19:11-27

List of Bible Stories with References	Text
2.4.3 Holy Week	
Triumphal Entry into Jerusalem	Mt 21:1-17; Mk 11:1-11; Lk 19:29-44
Barren Fig Tree Cursed	Mt 21:18-22; Mk 11:12-14, 20-24
Cleansing of Temple	Mt 21:15-17; Mk 11:15-18; Lk 19:45-48
Greeks Desire to See Jesus	Jn 12:20-50
Parables: Two Sons; Wicked Husbandmen; Marriage Feast of King's Son	Mt 21:28-22:14; Mk 11:27-12:12; Lk 20:1-19
Three Ensnaring Questions: Tribute to Caesar; Resurrection; Great Commandment	Mt 22:15-40; Mk 12:13-34; Lk 20:20-40
Jesus Gives Examples of Hypocrisy	Mt 23:13-36
Prophetic Words Spoken on Mt. of Olives	Mt 24:1 - 25:46
Parables: 10 Virgins; Talents; Separation of Sheep from Goats	Mt 25:1-46
Mary Anoints Jesus at Bethany	Mt 26:6-13; Jn 12:1-11
Judas Bargains with Rulers to Betray Jesus	Mt 26:14-16; Mk 14:10-11; Lk 22:3-6
Passover Meal	Mt 26:17-25; Mk 14:12-17; Lk 22:7-30
Jesus Washes Disciples' Feet	Jn 13:1-17
Jesus Predicts Judas' Betrayal and Peter's Denial	Mt 26:21-35; Mk 14:18-31; Jn 13:21-38
Lord's Supper Instituted	Mt 26:26-29; Mk 14:22-25; Lk 22:17-23; 1 Cor 11:23-26
Jesus' Farewell Discourse	Jn 14, 15, 16
Jesus' Intercessory Prayer	Jn 17
In Gethsemane: Jesus Prays and Is Arrested	Mt 26:36-56; Mk 14:32-52; Lk 22:39-53
Peter Denies His Lord	Mt 26:69-75; Mk 14:66-72; Jn 18:15-27
Jesus' Judgments	Mk 26:57- 27: 31; Mk 14:53 - 15:20; Lk 22:63 - 23:25; Jn 18:12- 19: 16

List of Bible Stories with References	Text
Jesus' Crucifixion, Death, Burial, and Guards at Tomb	Mt 27:32-65; Mk 15:21-46; Lk 23:26-56; Jn 19:17-42
2.5 Resurrected Life of Jesus	
Resurrection	Mt 28:1-15; Mk 16; Lk 24:1-12
Jesus with Mary Magdalene	Jn 20:11-17
Jesus with Two Disciples on Road to Emmaus	Lk 24:13-31
Jesus Appears to Disciples with Thomas Absent	Lk 24:36-43; Jn 20:19-25
Jesus Appears to the Disciples with Thomas Present	Jn 20:26-31
Miraculous Catch of Fish; Peter Reinstated	Jn 21:1-24
Great Commission	Mt 28:16-20; Mk 16:15-18; Ac 1:6-8
Last Appearance and Ascension	Lk 24:44-53; Ac 1:9-12
Second Coming of Jesus	Mt 24:27-31; Ac 1:10-11; Rev 1:7-8
3. Events in the Life of the Early Church	
Holy Spirit Comes at Pentecost	Acts 2:1-13
Peter's Message	2:14-40
First Converts	2:37-45
Crippled Beggar Healed	3:1-10
Peter and John Before the Sanhedrin	4:1-21
Believers Share Possessions	4:32-37
Ananias and Sapphira	5:1-11
Seven Helpers Chosen	6:1-7
Stephen: Seized; Tried; Stoned	6:8 - 7:66
Philip, the Evangelist	8:4-40
Saul's Conversion	9:1-18
Dorcas Restored to Life	9:36-43
Peter and Cornelius	10:1 - 11:18
Church in Antioch Begins	11:19-30
Peter Liberated from Prison	12:1-18
First Missionaries: Barnabas and Saul	13:1-4
In Lystra: Crippled Healed; Paul Stoned	14:8-20

List of Bible Stories with References	Text
Council at Jerusalem	15:1-21
Paul and Barnabas Separate	15:36-41
Vision of Man from Macedonia	16:6-10
In Philipi: Conversions and Prison	16:11-46
Paul in Athens	17:16-34
In Ephesus: Apollos; Paul Teaches; Miracles; Riot	18:18 - 19:41
Youth Falls from Window	20:7-12
Paul's Farewell to Ephesian Leaders	20:13-36
Paul Arrested in Temple	21:27-36
Paul Defends Himself	21:39 - 23:11
Paul Before King Agrippa	25:13-32
Paul in Storm at Sea	27:13-44
Paul Preaches at Rome under Guard	28:11-30
Paul's Message	1 Cor 2:1-5
Division in Church at Corinth	1 Cor 1:1-17
Paul Opposes Peter at Antioch	Gal 2:11-14
Paul's Struggles for Church	Col 1:24 - 2:5

LIST OF MIRACLES
In Chronological Order

1. MIRACLES IN THE OLD TESTAMENT
Miracles in the Old Testament are grouped in three distinct time periods.

1.1 The Liberating of the People of God from Egypt and Their Establishment in Canaan
- Ten Plagues .... Exodus 7-12
- Crossing the Red Sea .... Ex 14:21-31
- Bitter Waters at Marah Transformed .... Ex 15:22-27
- God Sends Manna .... Ex 16:1-36
- Water from the Rock at Rephidim .... Ex 17:1-7
- The Death of Nadab and Abihu .... Leviticus 10:1-5
- The Budding of Aaron's Staff .... Numbers 17
- Balaam and the Talking Donkey .... Num 22:22-35
- Crossing through the Jordan River .... Joshua 3:14-17
- Sun Stands Still .... Jos 10:1-14

1.2 The Conflict Against Pagan Religions, Led by Elijah and Elisha
- Elijah and the Drought .... 1 Kings 17:1-7
- Elijah and the Widow at Zarephath .... 1 Kin 17:8-24
- Elijah and Prophets of Baal on Mount Carmel ..... 1 Kin 18:1-46
- Soldiers Killed by Fire from Heaven .... 2 Kings 1:1-18
- Elijah Taken up to Heaven in a Chariot of Fire .... 2 Kin 2:1-18
- Water is Purified by Elisha .... 2 Kin 2:19-22
- Elisha Multiplied Oil for Widow .... 2 Kin 4:1-7
- Elisha Restored Shunammite's Son to Life .... 2 Kin 4:8-37
- Naaman Healed of Leprosy .... 2 Kin 5:1-19
- Elisha Makes an Ax-head Float .... 2 Kin 6:1-7
- Jonah and the Fish .... Jonah 1:15-2:10

1.3 The Time of Daniel, During the Exile in Babylon, When the Superiority of God Eternal above Other Gods, and the Faithfulness of Daniel and His Friends Was Vindicated
- The Faithful Servants of God in Fiery Furnace .... Daniel 3:1-31
- Daniel in Lions' Den .... Dan 6:1-28

2. MIRACLES IN THE NEW TESTAMENT
Matthew; Mark; Luke; John; Acts

2.1 THE MIRACLES OF JESUS IN CHRONOLOGICAL ORDER

2.1.1 Miracles Performed During the First Year of Ministry
- Water Transformed into Wine . . . . Jn 2:1-11
- Official's Son Cured from a Distance . . . . Jn 4:46-54

2.1.2 Miracles Performed During the Second Year of Ministry
- First Miraculous Catch of Fish . . . . Lk 5:3-11
- Jesus Drove Out an Evil Spirit at Capernaum . . . . . Mk 1:23-26; Lk 4:33-35
- Peter's Mother-in-law Healed .Mt 8:14-15; Mk 1:30-31; Lk 4:38-39
- Man with Leprosy Touched and Healed . . . . Mt 8:2-4; Mk 1:40-45; Lk 5:12-15
- Paralytic Lowered through the Roof . . . . . . Mt 9:1-8: Mk 2:1-12; Lk 5:17-26
- Invalid Cured on Sabbath at Pool . . . . Jn 5:1-9
- Man with a Shriveled Hand Cured on Sabbath . . . . . Mt 12:9-14; Mk 3:1-6; Lk 6:6-11
- Centurion's Servant Healed . . . . Mt 8:5-13: Lk 7:1-10
- Jesus Restored Widow's Son to Life . . . . Lk 7:11-17
- Blind, Mute Demon-possessed Man Healed . . . . . . Mt 12:22-37; Mk 3:12-30
- Jesus Calmed Storm at Sea Mt 8:23-27; Mk 4:35- 41; Lk 8:26-30
- Demon-possessed Man Healed and Pigs Drowned . Mt 8:28-34; Mk 5:1-20; Lk 8:26-39
- Bleeding Woman Healed . . Mt 9:20-22; Mk 5:23-34; Lk 8:43-48
- Jairus' Daughter Restored to Life . . . . Mt 9:18-34; Mk 5:21-24, 35-43; Lk 8:40-56
- Two Blind Men Healed . . . . Mt 9:27-31
- Mute Demon-possessed Man Healed . . . . Mt 9:32-33

2.1.3 Miracles Performed During the Third Year of Ministry
- Five Thousand Fed . . . . Mt 14:14-21; Mk 6:30-44; Lk 9:10-17; Jn 6:1-14
- Jesus Walked on Water . . Mt 14:24-33; Mk 6:47-52; Jn 6:15-21

- Syrophoenician Woman's Daughter Healed . . . . . . Mt 15:27-28; Mk 7:24-30
- Deaf and Mute Man Healed . . . . Mk 7:31-37
- Four Thousand Fed . . . . Mt 15:32-38; Mk 8:1-9
- Blind Man at Bethsaida Healed . . . . Mk 8:22-26
- Demon-possessed Boy Healed . . . . . . Mt 17:14-20; Mk 9:14-29; Lk 9:37-43
- Coin in Mouth of a Fish . . . . Mt 17:12-27
- Man Who Was Born Blind Healed . . . . Jn 9:1-41
- Crippled Woman Healed on Sabbath . . . . Lk 13:10-21
- Man with Dropsy Healed on Sabbath . . . . Lk 14:1-4
- Jesus Raised Lazarus from the Dead . . . . Jn 11:1-44
- Ten Healed of Leprosy . . . . Lk 17:11-19
- Blind Bartimaeus Received Sight . . . . Mt 20:29-34; Mk 10:45-52; Lk 18:35-43
- Fig Tree Cursed and Withered . . . . . . Mt 21:18-19; Mk 11:12-14
- Malchus' Cut-Off Ear Restored . . . . Lk 22:49-51; Jn 18:10-11

2.1.4 Miracle Performed During Jesus' Resurrected Life

- Second Miraculous Catch of Fish . . . . Jn 21:5-11

2.2 Miracles Performed During the Time of the Early Church
- Peter Healed Crippled Beggar . . . . Acts 3:1-10
- Ananias and Sapphira . . . . Ac 5:1-11
- Peter Healed Aeneas, a Paralytic . . . . Ac 9:32-36
- Peter Restored Dorcas to Life . . . . Ac 9:37-43
- Peter's Miraculous Release from Prison . . . . Ac 12:6-19
- Paul Healed Crippled Man in Lystra . . . . Ac 14:8-11
- Demon-possessed Fortune-teller Cured . . . . Ac 16:16-18
- Earthquake Released Paul and Silas from Prison . . . Ac 16:19-34
- Handkerchiefs from Paul Cured Sick . . . . Ac 19:11-12
- Youth Who Fell from Window Restored to Life . . . . . . Ac 20:7-12

LIST OF JESUS' PARABLES

1. **The Conflict of the New and the Old** (First Year of Ministry)
   - Guest of the Bridegroom . . . . Mt 9:14-15; Mk 2:18-20; Lk 5:33-35
   - New Patch and Old Garment. . . . . Mt 9:16; Mk 2:21; Lk 5:36
   - New Wine and Old Wineskin . . . . . Mt 9:17; Mk 2:22; Lk 5:37-39
   - Treasures, New and Old. . . . . Mt 13:51-52

2. **Wisdom is Proved by Action** (Second Year of Ministry)
   - Children at Play. Mt 11:16-19; Lk 7:31-35
   - Wise and Foolish Builders. . . . . Mt 7:24-27; Lk 6:46-49

3. **Nature and Development of the Kingdom** (Third Year of Ministry)
   - Sower and the Soils. . . . . Mt 13:3-8; Mk 4:4-8; Lk 8:5-8
   - Weeds Sowed Among Wheat. . . . . Mt 13:24-30, 36-43
   - Mustard Seed . . . . Mt 13:31-32; Mk 4:30-32; Lk 13:18-19
   - Yeast . . . . Mt 13:33; Lk 13:20-21
   - Hidden Treasure . . . . Mt 13:44
   - Pearl of Great Value . . . . Mt 13:45-46
   - Net that Caught All Kinds of Fish . . . . Mt 13:47-50
   - Growing Seed: Spontaneous Growth. . . . . Mk 4:26-29

4. **Counting the Cost of Discipleship**
   - Empty House (Second Year of Ministry). . . . . Mt 12:43-45
   - Uncompleted Tower (Third Year of Ministry). . . . . . . Lk 14:25-30
   - King's Rash Warfare (Third Year of Ministry) . . . . . . Lk 14:31-33

5. **Forgiven and Forgiving**
   - Two Debtors (Second Year of Ministry). . . . . Lk 7:36-43
   - Unmerciful Debtor (Third Year of Ministry) . . . . Mt 18:23-25

6. **Prayer** (Third Year of Ministry)
   - Persistent Friend at Midnight . . . . Lk 11:5-8
   - Persistent Widow. . . . . Lk 18:1-8

7. **Love for One's Neighbor** (Third Year of Ministry)
   - Good Samaritan . . . . Lk 10:30-37

8. **Humility** (Third Year of Ministry)
   - Chief Seats . . . . Lk 14:7-11
   - Pharisee and Tax Collector . . . . Lk 18:9-14

9. **Resourcefulness and Foresight** (Second Year of Ministry)
- Unjust Steward . . . . Lk 16:1-9

10. **Worldly Riches** (Second Year of Ministry)
- Rich Fool . . . . Lk 12:16-21
- Great Banquet . . . . Lk 14:16-24
- Rich Man and Beggar . . . . Lk 16:19-31

11. **Lost and Found** (Third Year of Ministry)
- Lost Sheep . . . . Mt 18:12-14; Lk 15:3-7
- Lost Coin . . . . Lk 15:8-10
- Prodigal Son . . . . Lk 15:11-24
- Elder Son Remained Outside the Party. . . . . Lk 15:25-31

12. **Service and Reward** (Third Year of Ministry)
- Workers in Vineyard . . . . Mt 20:1-16
- Talents (Passion Week). . . . . Mt 25:14-30
- Ten Minas of Gold . . . . Lk 19:11-27
- Unworthy Servants . . . . Lk 17:7-10

13. **Watching for the Return of Jesus** (Third Year of Ministry; Passion Week)
- Ten Virgins: Wise and Foolish Bridesmaids . . . . Mt 25:1-13
- Faithful and Unfaithful Servant . . . . Mt 24:45-51; Lk 12:41-48
- Watchful Door Keeper . . . . Mk 13:32-37

14. **The Kingdom and Judgment** (Third Year of Ministry; Passion Week)
- Two Sons . . . . Mt 21:28-32
- Evil Tenants . . . . Mt 21:33-34; Mk 12:1-12; Lk 20:9-18
- Unproductive Fig Tree . . . . Lk 13:6-9
- Rejected Cornerstone. . . . . Mt 21:42-45
- Wedding Banquet of King's Son . . . . Mt 22:1-14
- Separating Sheep from Goats. . . . . Mt 25:14-46

www.ingramcontent.com/pod-product-compliance
Lightning Source LLC
Chambersburg PA
CBHW070643160426
43194CB00009B/1562